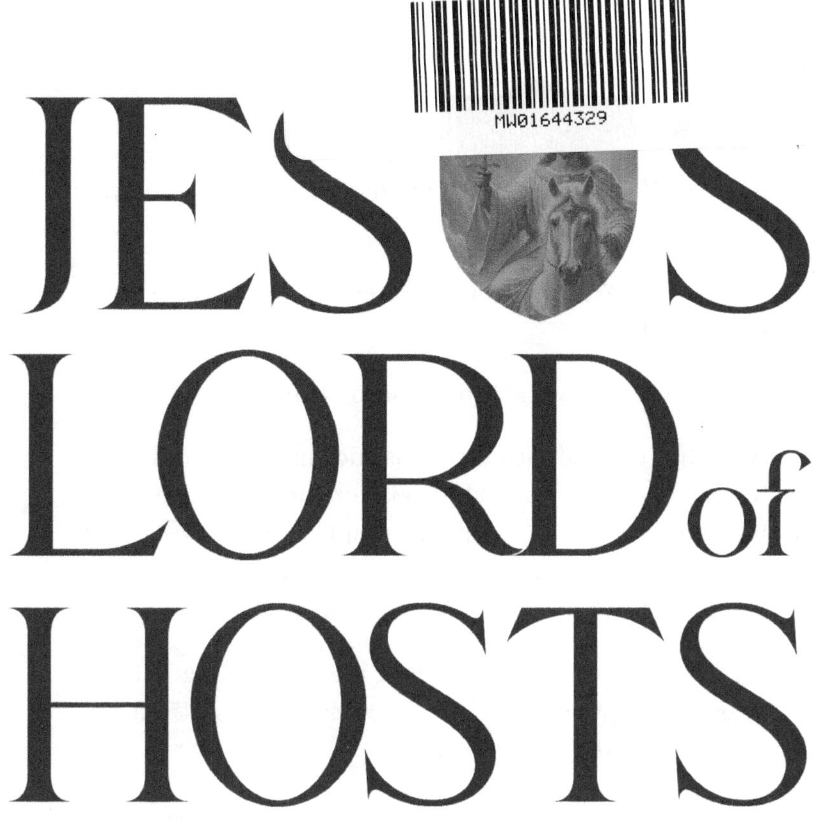

JESUS LORD of HOSTS

Discovering Christ as Commander of Heaven's Armies in the Old Testament, Today, and at His Return

BLAKE LORENZ

Author of *Greater Love*

Jesus, Lord of Hosts: Discovering Christ as Commander of Heaven's Armies in the Old Testament, Today and at His Return

This title is also available on Amazon Kindle.

Published by World Evangelism Center Orlando

Cover and interior design:
Kristi Griffith, Thumbprint Creative Arts

Paperback ISBN: 979-8-9992846-0-0

Digital ISBN: 979-8-9992846-1-7

DEDICATION

I dedicate this book to the memory of Christ Bright.

For more than forty years Chris was one of the most remarkable ministry partners I was blessed to know. After falling in love with Christ in the mountains of Guatemala, he dedicated his life to the gospel.

Together, we shared the love of Jesus in Guatemala, the Congo, Zambia, and the streets of Orlando. He helped me write books, produce podcasts, and served as President of Blake Lorenz Evangelism Ministries, which later became World Evangelism Center Orlando.

Before he went home to heaven in 2024, he helped with the first two chapters of this book and told me to "get her done." His encouragement still fuels me. I know Jesus welcomed him with the words, "Well done, good and faithful servant."

Chris, keep a tee time ready for me—after all, you're just five minutes ahead. See you soon at the feet of Jesus.

PROCEEDS WITH PURPOSE

All net proceeds from this book are being donated to the World Evangelism Center Orlando to support their global mission and ministry.

Our Mission:

To prepare the way for Jesus's Second Coming by calling people to repent and believe in Jesus Christ, to be baptized with the Holy Spirit and fire, to deny self, take up their cross, and follow Jesus.

Our Vision:

To go to the church, to Israel, and the nations to establish World Evangelism Centers around the globe in order to plant churches and spread the salvation of Jesus Christ, and to see all believers baptized with the Holy Spirit and fire.

To learn more or support directly, visit worldevangelismcenterorlando.org.

TABLE OF CONTENTS

TO THE READER

This book is grounded in the biblical account and supported by historical and cultural context. In some sections, logical inferences are made based on what is recorded in Scripture, what is known about the historical period, and what would be considered normal human responses. Certain scenes—such as inner thoughts, emotional responses, and interactions not directly recorded in Scripture—are imaginatively reconstructed to reflect the experiences of Jesus and the prophets, always with the intent to remain faithful to what could have plausibly occurred.

Additionally, personal stories included in this book are based on the author's memories and experiences. They are shared to illustrate spiritual truths and are presented as remembered to the best of the author's ability.

All Scripture referenced is from the New King James Version.

INTRODUCTION

The Revelations That Changed Everything

In 1992, my wife Beverly and I were pastoring a small Methodist church in Orlando when we were invited to a James Robison conference. We were just beginning to embrace the Spirit-led life, but I felt I was too busy to attend. Beverly knew we needed to go.

That decision changed everything.

The first speaker was Jack Hayford, a man I'd never heard of. But when he preached, I prayed, *"Whatever he has, I want it."* Jack shared how his small congregation outside Los Angeles had prayed for God's presence—and how God responded with a cloud of glory. That presence grew the church to thousands, and Jack's ministry reached millions.

But what stayed with me most was a vision Jack described: Jesus, dressed as our High Priest, rising from His throne, oil flowing over the nations. And the Father declaring, *"My Son is rising to prepare the world for His return."*

The Spirit prompted me to lie prostrate before God. I resisted at first, not wanting to seem out of order. Then James Robison walked to the microphone and said, "I believe God is calling us to come and lie before Him."

Wham! Along with hundreds of others, I ran to the front. The Spirit poured out as on the Day of Pentecost. I lay there for nearly thirty minutes receiving the anointing to preach to the nations and proclaim the return of Jesus

Christ. God told me that He would use me to bring revival to Methodists.

I asked the Spirit, "*Who am I to go?*" I was at a tiny church, unknown and unproven. God took care of that because He began sending me to local churches and then overseas. The true revival was in the Methodist churches in Zambia and Cuba, which I have been blessed to be a part of since 2000. We have witnessed "Book of Acts" miracles and incredible growth.

Little did I know then that this Spirit-filled encounter would mark the beginning of a journey that eventually led me to a deeper revelation—one that has reshaped my understanding of Jesus and the role He plays in Scripture and in our world. That revelation is this: *Jesus Christ is the Lord of Hosts.*

It's a title many skim past in Scripture, yet its significance is profound. *Lord of Hosts*—Yahweh Sabaoth—means Commander of Heaven's Armies. And that Commander is Jesus. Understanding this truth changed how I read the Bible, how I face trials, and how I live with hope and confidence in these chaotic times. It's the reason I wrote this book.

The Message and the Mission

In these pages, you're invited to:

- Understand the profound connection between the title *Lord of Hosts* and Jesus Christ. Every mention of the *Lord of Hosts* refers to Jesus, meaning He is the Commander of God's heavenly armies. Recognizing the connection reshapes how we view His role in prophecy, history, and our lives.

- Explore the prophecies in Isaiah and their fulfillment through Jesus Christ. These ancient words, written over 2,700 years ago, reveal God's plan for Israel's redemption, humanity's salvation, and the ultimate unveiling of His purpose for the world.

- Apply the truth of Jesus as *Lord of Hosts* to present-day challenges. In a world of uncertainty and conflict, understanding Jesus as the protector, deliverer, and source of eternal hope offers a foundation for living with courage, purpose, and faith.

Since stepping into the Spirit-led life over thirty years ago, I've witnessed God do what only He can do. Through World Evangelism Center Orlando, the ministry He entrusted to us, we are now reaching over 150 nations and seeing around ten thousand come to Christ monthly. These are not merely statistics—they are living testimonies to the power and authority of Jesus Christ, the *Lord of Hosts.*

Why It Matters Now

The October 7, 2023, attacks on Israel and escalating global conflicts have prompted me to share why this message matters now. In fragile times like these, Isaiah's writings take on a new urgency. They foreshadow the unveiling described in Revelation, revealing what was, what is, and what is to come. If these prophecies are true—and I believe they are—they challenge us to live with purpose, be prepared for the chaos of world events, and stand firm in the truth of who Jesus is.

Each chapter of this book includes questions for personal reflection or group discussion. Whether you're reading alone or with others, I hope that you'll come away with renewed confidence in Christ's sovereignty and love.

Jesus Christ is not only Savior—He is the protector of God's people, the Deliverer from evil, the Judge of creation, and the One who bestows God's greatest gifts on those who believe.

Let's begin this journey together. Anchored in Scripture, guided by the Spirit, and grounded in the truth of Jesus, the *Lord of Hosts.*

1

The Vision

It was no ordinary Saturday morning. It was a holiday–Sukkot–a joyful celebration where Jewish families and communities come together to commemorate God's provision during the Israelites' journey in the wilderness. Sukkahs, temporary shelters, were decorated with colorful paper chains and greenery. Soldiers were home on leave to share meals and blessings with their families. Prayers of gratitude filled neighborhood synagogues as they marked the special occasion.

It was no ordinary Saturday morning. A nation known for its incredible vigilance born out of the necessity of being surrounded by enemies that wish to erase them was caught off guard. In that moment of vulnerability, one thousand Hamas terrorists invaded Israel and unleashed a spree of murder, torture and rape. Civilians were "massacred in at least 14 Israeli towns and communities. The scenes of horror and bloodshed that resulted—the murder of entire families, the kidnapping of small children, and rape of young women, were intended to cause maximum anger and shock inside Israel." [1] Throughout their rampage, they shouted Allāhu Akbar, God is Great.

The death toll for the small country was 1,200. [2] To put that in perspective, it would be as if over 30,000 people were killed in the U.S. in one day. [3] "Some victims were tortured, raped, burned, and mutilated, with many of the acts filmed by the perpetrators. The attackers also killed hundreds of soldiers situated near the border." [4] [5] At the Supernova Music Festival, 360 young people were butchered to death, and another 240 were taken hostage.

Accounts of babies burned in ovens and cut from their mother's wombs [6] illustrate the extent of evil the Hamas terrorists, supported and encouraged by Iran, are willing to carry out. They committed these atrocities in the guise of deserved revenge. In reality, they are driven by the inner beast of humanity.

I met Joel*, an Israeli Defense Force (IDF) soldier, as he wandered through a kibbutz along the Gaza border and took in this nightmare. Somber, heartbroken, and enraged. The carnage was incomprehensible, as was the feeling of being abandoned by the world. Joel wondered, "Where is the media? The BBC, ABC, FOX…Why aren't they present to tell the world about this twenty-first-century Holocaust?"

Joel observed the bullet holes that decimated homes. The intent was obvious–destroy any vestige of civility. He compassionately listened as a survivor told him that Palestinian workers who came across the Gaza border

*Joel is a pseudonym.

daily to find work gave Hamas details, enabling the terrorists to maximize pain and chaos. They knew the kibbutz residents turned their rifles into the armory each night. So, in an act of sheer cowardice, they stationed snipers to shoot the men and women as they ran out to retrieve their weapons. Left defenseless, innocent babies, children, and adults were brutalized, tortured, killed, or kidnapped. Like the survivor, Joel wondered how those the community had befriended could turn on them.

The evils of October 7, 2023, were recorded on the attackers' video cams and cell phones of those under attack. The world cannot deny what happened.

Isaiah: A Man of Vision

Isaiah was a man of vision. He predicted Israel's present-day horrors 2700 years ago in Isaiah chapters 1-12. He also prophesied that the *Lord of Hosts* would come to defend God's people and destroy those who oppose His plan of salvation.

But who is the *Lord of Hosts*—Yahweh Sabaoth—*that* Isaiah refers to around 60 times? It's actually a phrase that appears over 200 times in the Bible. Emphasizing Jesus's sovereign rule over heaven and earth.

He is the Commander of the hosts, heaven's armies made up of angels, sent to accomplish God's purposes and protect His people. It's a title that emphasizes Jesus's authority over nations and armies.

This same Commander is present throughout Scripture, with Isaiah's vision being part of a larger story. The Bible outlines this vision through centuries of prophetic words, beginning with Adam in the Garden of Eden, when God promised that the offspring of the woman, ultimately fulfilled in Jesus Christ, would defeat Satan (Genesis 3:15).

God sent Isaiah powerful revelations to speak to His people about the terror they faced and the hope of salvation. Through the prophet, God revealed His plan to save a remnant of the Jews so that His Son could be born in Bethlehem, in the region of Judea, in the land of Israel.

The apostle John later confirms Isaiah's visions in John 12:37-41, quoting Isaiah 6:8-9. He identifies the *Lord of Hosts* that Isaiah saw in the temple as Jesus Christ. This connection emphasizes that the same Jesus who came to save the world had already been working through the prophecies and warnings given to Isaiah centuries earlier.

Isaiah's warnings were clear: judgment was coming as a consequence of disobedience and their refusal to repent. The northern kingdom of Israel would fall. Its people would be scattered, and genealogies blurred by intermarriage with the Assyrians. Judea would also face invasion, and city after city would fall to the evil Assyrian Empire. Jerusalem stood alone as a final outpost of hope.

In the writings of Isaiah, we discover insight and application into modern-day Israel and our global chaos, where we find ourselves in a world that often feels like we are on the verge of World War III. The parallels between Isaiah's prophecies and modern events are striking. In Isaiah 5:20, the prophet warns, "Woe to those who call evil good and good evil..." reflecting the moral confusion experienced because of ancient and present-day conflicts.

Similarly, Isaiah 13:11 states, "I will punish the world for its evil, the wicked for their sins…" echoing the consequences of unchecked violence and hatred. Nevertheless, amid these warnings, Isaiah also delivered God's promises. His writings point to a future redemption through the Messiah, not just for Israel but for all nations. His message speaks to our times, offering insight into the chaos of our modern world and the hope we find in Christ.

Jesus: *Lord of Hosts*

To emphasize the prophecies of Isaiah, we only have to look at ourselves in the church. Almost weekly, we hear of scandals in the leadership of the church. How can pastors preach, lead TV ministries, write books, and record podcasts about Jesus, and still be involved in child molestation, extramarital affairs, rape, or fraud?

These leaders profess powerful faith in Jesus Christ, yet indulge in terrible sin without any public repentance. Some even deny wrongdoing. However, the evidence and testimonies of those they harmed expose their wickedness.

Is this any different from the Jews of Isaiah's day who proclaimed faith in the God of Abraham, yet they were consumed with idolatry by worshiping false gods? Isaiah's message was to repent and return to God, to trust in the *Lord of Hosts* alone for their salvation.

While pondering this issue, my wife, Beverly, a powerful woman of God who believes in the sacred call to holiness, gave me this answer. The success of their ministries had become their false gods. Instead of repenting, they must defend themselves against these accusations. The accolades, wealth, and success become their gods. Therefore, they must defend their character to prevent losing power, money, and prestige.

Is this not the same idolatry that Isaiah called his people to repent from? Our Lord calls us to godly sorrow, repentance that leads to life, not worldly sorrow that leads to death. Like the Jews in Isaiah 1, who defended their faith in God yet were evil, have we also become blind to the truth and deaf to the conviction of the Holy Spirit?

Jesus will say to those who perform great miracles in His name but didn't remain faithful to Him, "Depart from Me. I never knew you." We can only serve one master; we can't serve God and riches. The refusal of church leaders to repent declares which god they serve—the same as the ancient Jews in Samaria and Judea.

When Beverly shared the revelation about church leaders who do not repent, I was led to study the life of Judas. He followed Jesus as one of His twelve apostles. He witnessed miracles and crowds amazed at Jesus's teaching. Judas knew Jesus to be a man who loved the unlovable and forgave sins. Jesus patiently discipled Judas and the other eleven to do what He did. My impression is that Judas believed in Jesus as the Messiah. Nevertheless, in the end, he tried to force Jesus's hand to overthrow the Romans and set up His kingdom.

Judas sold out Jesus to the Pharisees for thirty pieces of silver. Yes, he believed in Jesus while serving other gods. Have these leaders, like Judas, sold out their faith for the riches and fame of this world? Have they exchanged their eternal destiny for temporary treasures to gain the world and lose their soul?

The message from Isaiah resounds in our day: Jesus is coming. Like the red thread of truth connecting Genesis to Revelation, the only hope of salvation is to trust in Jesus Christ alone, the *Lord of Hosts.* Do not fool yourself into trusting anyone or anything else.

When we discover that we have been trusting in other gods or things along with Jesus, we should repent as David did in Psalm 51. Throw yourself upon the mercy and grace of Jesus Christ and ask forgiveness. Receive His forgiveness by His blood and seek to love and serve Him alone. Don't be afraid to lose your worldly reputation, riches, or position. Do not hold onto your sin; confess it and return to the *Lord of Hosts* as your One and Only Savior. Jesus will rebuild your life and draw you into His intimacy of love and redemption. Trust in Him alone. The *Lord of Hosts* is your only hope of salvation.

Holy Encounter: The Asbury Revival

For students at Asbury University, attending Wednesday morning chapel service is expected. They sing, pray, hear a message, and then, after the benediction, head to class. Yet, on February 8, 2023, many were overcome by what they described as "a quiet but powerful sense of transcendence, and they did not want to go. They stayed and continued to worship." [7]

The ordinary chapel service turned into a supernatural visitation of God. The students lingered, sensing the tangible presence of Jesus. What began as routine became a continuous outpouring of the Holy Spirit, lasting sixteen days and nights without interruption. People from across the nation and around the world flocked to Wilmore, Kentucky, seeking an encounter with the living Christ.

This revival was not unprecedented. Asbury University has long been a place where revivals have broken out, shaping generations of students and sending them out to proclaim Jesus. At its heart, Asbury has always carried a vision for holiness—a life fully surrendered to God, cleansed from sin, and empowered by the Holy Spirit. This foundational belief, often called entire sanctification, was central to the teachings of John Wesley and has marked every major revival in the school's history, including those in 1950 and 1970.

Wanting to witness the revival firsthand, my wife, Beverly, and I traveled to Asbury. We made our way to the chapel, where lines of people stretched outside, waiting hours to enter. People from all walks of life—students, pastors, families with children, and elderly–were willing to wait as long as it took. Even across the street at the Seminary Chapel, overflow crowds gathered as the services were broadcast from the college chapel.

Because of my past work writing for Charisma's online magazine, we were given access to the services as journalists, allowing us to bypass the long lines and sit in the front row. From the moment we stepped inside, the presence of God was undeniable.

Worship was led mostly by students without a structured plan or program, yet the movement of the Holy Spirit was powerful. Some stood with hands raised, lost in reverence, while others knelt at the altar, weeping in repentance. There was no formal plan, no famous speakers—only people with holy desperation for Jesus.

At several moments, the congregation was asked to stand in public repentance or gather in small circles for prayer. The altar was rarely empty—people of all ages knelt before God, surrendering everything. No human could have orchestrated such an authentic movement. It was a divine visitation. On the wall beneath the cross, large letters proclaim: HOLINESS UNTO THE LORD. It was the perfect description of what we were experiencing.

In today's church, holiness often takes a backseat to self-fulfillment and secular humanism. This revival was a call to return to a life wholly surrendered to Jesus, a life where repentance is not just a moment but a way of walking with God.

This movement was not about an emotional experience—it was a call back to the heart of God. As we left the chapel each day, we weren't just inspired; we were transformed. The revival did not end when the students returned to class. It sparked something that continued to spread across college campuses and beyond.

Asbury: A Legacy of Holiness

My connection to Asbury runs deep. My father-in-law, John Brackman, encountered Jesus through the 1950 Asbury revival. At the time, he was a rebellious preacher's kid, uninterested in the things of God. However, when

Asbury students came to testify at his father's church in Georgia, the presence of God was so strong that he and his brother couldn't resist it. That night, both surrendered to Jesus along with their two younger brothers. All four became holiness preachers, United Methodist ministers who sought to lead by the example of John Wesley, emphasizing sanctification and complete devotion to God.

The impact of that revival didn't just change their family—it led thirty-four men from their small church into full-time ministry. The 1970 Asbury revival also transformed Beverly. At just 13 years old, she was so moved by the testimonies that she organized witness teams in her church, sending them out every Sunday night to share the gospel. Her devotion to Jesus and the call to holiness have shaped her life. She is a mighty woman of God and an outstanding Bible teacher with an unwavering love for Christ.

Then, in 1980, after I encountered Jesus, I was led to John's church in Winter Park, Florida. Under his leadership, I began understanding Jesus's vision for my life. When I told him I felt led to attend seminary, he simply said, *"Your only choice is Asbury Seminary."*

Returning to Asbury in 2023 felt like stepping into the very legacy of holiness that had shaped our lives. This revival was not about nostalgia or religious tradition—it was about the living power of God transforming hearts today.

As we left Asbury, we carried a renewed vision. This revival was not about a moment in time; it was a call for believers everywhere to return to holiness, to embrace the baptism of the Holy Spirit, and to live as true disciples of Christ.

The fire that fell in Wilmore, Kentucky, is still burning, igniting a new generation to live fully surrendered to Jesus.

After our experience at Asbury, I returned to the book of Isaiah for perhaps the hundredth time. Yet, this time was different. I sensed the Spirit telling me to see Isaiah's words through the lens of Jesus Christ as the *Lord of Hosts*, the Commander of God's armies. While I understood the book's prophecies for Judea and Israel, I could see Jesus's actions in the days of Isaiah, into the future of modern-day Israel, and then to the Second Coming of Christ.

The revelation flowed together in the first eleven chapters of Isaiah, and I was inspired to write this book on the *Lord of Hosts*. Jesus is alive in every chapter. I saw a view of history new to me, especially leading up to the October 7, 2023 massacre and the return of Jesus as the coming Ruler, the Prince of Peace.

A whole new picture of prophecy unfolded: Jesus working in God's redemption plan through the history of Israel, then and now, and into our future. The wonder of this revelation awakened me to a deeper passion concerning the return of Jesus, the season in which we now live, and how we should prepare the way for His return.

Isaiah speaks of the *Lord of Hosts* about 60 times. Here are others who wrote of the *Lord of Hosts* leading the people of God to His vision.

Haggai - 14 times	Amos - 6 times
Zechariah - 53 times	Jeremiah - 82 times

Jesus: The Ultimate Visionary

In Him, we see the full character of the *Lord of Hosts*: the holiness that awed Isaiah, the authority that stilled storms and cast out demons, and the fearless power that challenged corrupt religious leaders and confronted the forces of darkness (Matthew 23; John 2:13-17).

He was also the greatest visionary to ever live. Long before His earthly ministry, Jesus revealed Himself to Isaiah in a vision—holy, exalted, and glorious. Later, during His time in Israel, He gave the people a new vision of how to live: a life that loved, honored, and pleased God.

His mission, given by His Father in heaven, was for His followers to make disciples of all nations (Matthew 28:18-19). They were to proclaim the greatest news ever given: the free gift of salvation through Jesus's sacrifice.

Jesus's vision for humanity was one of transformation. He called people to repent, put their faith in Him, and live lives that honored God. His teachings—especially the Sermon on the Mount—outlined a new way of life centered on love, humility, and obedience to God's will.

The only way people can do God's will on earth and be saved from their sins is by faith in Him alone. They must put away their old way of life and live His new way, which He teaches in the Sermon on the Mount (Matthew Chapters 5 - 7). I will attempt to summarize the greatest teaching ever given to humanity. Much of what I learned from the Sermon on the Mount came from a book by E. Stanley Jones, *The Christ of the Mount*.

When first read, this radical teaching of Jesus is beautiful beyond any human ability to create. It seems impossible to live. Yet, when Jesus's truth burns in our hearts, we want to live out His vision for life as opposed to the religions of men. He plants the seeds of glory in us so we will reject the old visions of the world. Only Jesus and His righteousness can satisfy our souls.

Jesus opens the Sermon on the Mount by stating that God desires to bless us with eternal truths that reach far beyond earthly bounds. A picture of God is woven into His message. It is given practical life when reflected in Jesus, the God who became flesh to teach us His ways.

The ideal He presents takes us into heaven to remind us how and why God created us: to love our Creator, to love one another, and to love ourselves. It requires transformation within our being, as Jesus tells us our problem is that we are inwardly divided by trying to serve many masters. However, we were created to serve only God.

We need a heart transplant, which only the Holy Spirit can perform. Jesus calls us in Matthew 5:3 to be humble before God, "Blessed are the poor in spirit, for theirs is the kingdom of heaven." Dying to our selfishness enables us to be filled with the fullness of God. We can then reenter the world to share in the suffering of others. We are called to have a pure heart and be merciful, to be the salt and light of the world, so that we can bring hope and truth as His witnesses.

In the end, Jesus tells us we will be persecuted for His sake. Yet, we are to rejoice in our sacrifice. How do I rejoice when

I am mocked, betrayed, and ridiculed for my faith in Jesus? It's one of the hardest lessons I am still trying to learn.

Jesus closes the Sermon on the Mount with a stern warning. The storms of life will come. Therefore, be hearers and doers of His teaching. Those who only hear will not survive the storms of life. Those who do His words will last for eternity. The road to hell is wide and open, but the way to eternal and abundant life in this world is narrow. Choose Jesus and His vision of living, and know God and His peace. Choose the ways of men, and you will perish.

I encourage you to read, study, and memorize these teachings. Get a copy of *The Christ of the Mount* and use it as a Bible study guide for yourself and others. It will open your eyes and your heart to live as the *Lord of Hosts* created you to live.

Bartimaeus: A Vision Restored

The message of the Sermon on the Mount is transformative. One of the most profound examples of its powerful message is the story of blind Bartimaeus (Mark 10:46-52). Jesus was on His way to Jerusalem to die for us on the cross. He passed through the village of Jericho with His disciples. Crowds of people followed Him, hoping to hear Him speak and to see Him perform a miracle. They were hungry for a new way of life.

Bartimaeus, a blind man begging by the roadside, heard the commotion and asked what was happening. When he learned that Jesus was passing by, he cried out, "Son of David, have mercy on me!" Here was a man who had no physical or life vision. Bartimaeus lived a hopeless life, begging by the side of the road. He did not believe God loved him, nor could he love God. Yet, he called out to Jesus.

The crowd tried to silence him, dismissing him as unworthy of Jesus's attention. Bartimaeus, however, refused to be quiet. He cried out louder until Jesus stopped and said, "Bring him to Me."

When Bartimaeus stood before Him, Jesus asked, "What do you want Me to do for you?"

"Lord, I want to see," Bartimaeus replied.

With compassion, Jesus said, "Receive your sight; your faith has made you well." Instantly, Bartimaeus could see, and his life was forever changed. He joined the followers of Jesus, filled with purpose and hope.

This story illustrates Jesus's desire not only to heal physical blindness but also the even more profound meaning that He wants to give people a new vision for living. Bartimaeus went from being a hopeless beggar to a man with a purpose, transformed by Jesus's love and power.

The same Jesus who gave Isaiah visions and restored Bartimaeus's sight invites us to discover His vision for our lives. As Acts Chapter 2 tells us, the Holy Spirit gives believers dreams and visions to guide us in preparing for Jesus's return.

Jesus, as the *Lord of Hosts*, has the power to protect His people and lead them in fulfilling His Father's plan. Throughout Scripture, this title signifies His might and authority as the Commander of heaven's armies. He fights on our behalf, defending us from spiritual attacks and empowering us to carry out His mission.

Like Isaiah, we are called to respond to God's vision with faith and obedience. In Isaiah 6, after seeing the Lord seated on His throne and being cleansed from sin, the prophet heard the voice of the Lord asking, "Whom shall I send?" Isaiah's response—"Here I am, send me!"—remains an example for all who seek to serve God's purposes.

The vision Jesus gives us is not just for our benefit. It is to glorify God and share the hope of salvation with others. Through His death and resurrection, Jesus made a way for us to be reconciled to God. He offers us a life filled with meaning, purpose, and the promise of eternal life.

The Bell Ringer: A Call to Awaken

Our crusades in Zambia were almost over. For two weeks, we had been sharing Jesus and His salvation in villages on the edge of civilization. I was weary and had almost lost my voice. Yet, the cost was worth seeing God's miracle in these humble tribal people, as new souls were born into the kingdom.

We were in our last service in Kabompo village, where we planted a church years earlier. I planned to hold three services before returning home. As we finished our last meeting, I listened as the District Superintendent offered what were to be closing comments. Then, he looked at me and asked if we could have one more service that night since we were leaving the next day. He reminded me that God had moved mightily during our time there.

I looked down at the dirt floor, and my first thought was no. I had no strength left. My voice was gone. I had no more to give. Yet, when I looked up, I nodded yes. We had come from America to pour our lives out for Jesus and these people in Zambia. *How could I say no?*

The services were usually held late in the afternoon because there was no electricity. However, for this last service, we would meet after dinner in the dark. I arrived early at the pitch-black church to pray for God to give me the strength to preach and minister one last time.

As I entered the church, an older woman was sweeping the dirt floor, singing joyfully. What struck me, though, was not her singing. I recalled how she was stooped in pain when we first arrived. I asked her what had happened to cause such a transformation. She lit up and shouted God healed her. She danced up and down the aisle to demonstrate how God had set her free.

That was enough to inspire me to trust in Jesus that this would be a powerful service. And it was. As it neared its conclusion, many of the young singers came forward to repent, acknowledging they had been living two lives, one for Jesus and one for sin. The Holy Spirit fell, and we had a wonderful experience of repentance and salvation.

Exhausted, I asked everyone not to talk to me as I returned to my lodgings. All I wanted was to crawl under the mosquito netting and sleep.

Before daybreak, someone in the village began to ring the village bell. Bang, bang, bang, it peeled, waking me from my peaceful rest. It felt like the ringing was occurring in my head—bang, bang, bang.

"God, please make him stop. I just want to sleep." The noise continued as if the bell ringer's only job was to wake everyone in the village. On and on he rang as I begged God, "Make him stop," but the bell ringer was determined to get us all out of bed.

Then, the Holy Spirit spoke to me. "You have not heard this bell all week. I did this purposely this morning to wake you up. For Jesus is coming again, and My people are asleep. They just want to sit comfortably in their pews while the world is far from God. I want you to wake them up. Ring the bell! Ring the bell! Ring the bell!"

I took this message everywhere I went: Cuba, Zambia, Israel, Haiti, America, Congo, Malawi, Kenya, Pakistan… to the nations. At almost every meeting, the people would rise up, some even standing on their pews or chairs, shouting," Send me! Send me!" A mighty anointing fell upon us at each location.

In Zambia, many began to put bells on poles to ring as a reminder to wake up and call people to trust in Jesus Christ alone. This message has gone out to 188 nations through my podcast, television, conferences, and crusades. It is the same message Isaiah shared in Chapters 1-12. May we hear it today and act upon it by telling everyone to repent and to believe.

In the past 45 years, I have encountered the Resurrected Jesus in many ways. The experience in Kabompo, however, awakened me to the reality that Jesus is coming again soon. Thus, I'm highly motivated to call the church and the nations to wake up; our King is on His horse, ready to ride.

The *Lord of Hosts*: His Mission, Our Calling

As I reflect on the bell ringer waking the village, I can't help but see a parallel to the tragic events of October 7, 2023. That day was a wake-up call for Israel and for all who profess to follow Christ. Just as the kibbutz residents were caught off guard, many in the Church today remain spiritually complacent. Will we continue to sleep, or will we rise, repent, and stand as bold witnesses for the *Lord of Hosts*?

The good news is the *Lord of Hosts*, Jesus Christ, invites you to join His mission—to be part of the greatest vision ever given: the redemption of the world.

In these chapters, we will discover why Jesus is called the *Lord of Hosts* and what the title entails. We will learn about the inspired words given to Isaiah for his day, for the centuries following, even into our time, and into the future. Wake up! God has provided the blueprints for the times we live in. Those who follow Jesus Christ will know the hope of eternal life, and those who reject Him will experience eternal separation from God's love.

Before we move on, I challenge you to pray for the Holy Spirit to open your eyes as you read and complete the questions at the end of each chapter. May you get to know Jesus as the *Lord of Hosts*.

Enjoy the adventure of Jesus, Scripture, and the promise of our Lord's return in the context of what was, what is, and what will come. You may be surprised by how it will impact you as you apply the lessons of Isaiah to your life.

GOING DEEPER | Chapter 1

Reflect & Respond

1. Revival at Asbury University came through genuine repentance. Pray for the Holy Spirit to reveal areas you need to repent of. Write any that come to mind.

2. Read Proverbs 3:5-6, Isaiah 26:3-4, Matthew 6:33. How are these verses similar? Choose one of the verses to commit to memory and reflect on this week.

3. Bartimaeus was physically blind but cried out for Jesus to restore his sight (Mark 10:46-52). The chapter parallels spiritual blindness, where people—even those who claim to have faith—fail to see God's vision clearly. In what ways do you see spiritual blindness in the world today? Are there areas in your life where you need to ask Jesus to open your eyes to His truth and purpose?

4. The chapter ends with a powerful personal testimony about waking up to the urgency of Jesus's return. Isaiah also called Israel to repentance before judgment came. What would you say if you had to "ring the bell" and wake up those around you to the reality of Jesus's return? How can you personally live with greater urgency in preparing for His coming?

For Further Study & Discussion

1. The author shares how Jesus is the *Lord of Hosts*–Commander of Heaven's Armies. How does understanding Jesus as the *Lord of Hosts* change your view of Him and/or His role in biblical history?

2. Isaiah prophesied about judgment and redemption for Israel (Isaiah 1-12). The chapter connects this prophecy to modern events, particularly the October 7, 2023 attack on Israel.

   How does seeing these ancient prophecies unfold in present-day events impact your understanding of God's sovereignty and the accuracy of His Word?

3. Where do you see modern parallels to Israel's mistake of trusting in human power, wealth, or alliances instead of God? How can you personally ensure that your faith is fully in Jesus alone?

4. The chapter compares the idolatry of Israel in Isaiah's time to the failures of some modern church leaders whose ministries have become their false gods. What warning does this give you about the dangers of success, power, and self-justification?

   How can you guard yourself from making anything—even good things—an idol that replaces God?

5. Read Isaiah 6:8 and Acts 2:17-18. List ways God has given you direction, and describe how you responded.

History is a mirror, reflecting not just the choices of nations but the hearts of individuals. Like Israel, I, too, once walked in darkness. But the *Lord of Hosts* calls each of us by name, offering redemption before judgment comes.

The only question that remains: *Will we answer His call?*

2

The Refining

Sports was my God. I was raised in the church and was taught all about Jesus, but I never had much use for Him. My dream was to play centerfield for the New York Yankees, and by God's grace, I was a successful athlete. Although the Yankees offered to sign me after high school, I chose to attend college on a full scholarship.

Success came easily to me. My college baseball career won me the recognition of the Chicago Cubs organization. At age 21, I signed a contract with them. I thought I was on my way, but the Cubs eventually released me. I returned home filled with anger, despair, and hopelessness. Why was I ever born? Everything I had given my life to was gone. I had no purpose for living; my dreams were dead.

Night after night, I wallowed, consumed by my failure. My pain became so intense that one night, in desperation, I cried out to Jesus to take my life and use it for His glory. In that instant, He was in my room. For the first time in my life, I knew Jesus was real. He enveloped me with the most beautiful love I could imagine. My sins were forgiven and erased, and all my pain vanished. It was as though I was in heaven. I remember saying to Him, "Being with You is paradise." I just wanted to stay with Him forever, but He said, "No. I will send you to the nations to tell them of My love and salvation." I wasn't sure what He meant, but I was ready to find out.

From Failure to Purpose

When I woke up the next morning, I was a changed person. His love and presence transformed me. My life took on a new direction–to learn about Jesus. It took on a whole new purpose–to tell my story to people worldwide. My transformation led me to embrace the vital issues of life–salvation, grace, forgiveness, and the pursuit of knowing God's will. It also led me in the last 20 years to travel the globe and witness how God's love sets people free from the bondage of sin.

Looking back at my younger baseball days, I would have thought it was ludicrous for God to use me as an evangelist. However, as my gift for evangelism grew, so did my realization of the world's problems. On the one hand, I felt a profound sense of hope, while on the other, I became more aware of the pain and problems encountered daily.

As I grew in wisdom, I realized that a solution can't be found until the problem is acknowledged. The tumultuous history of the Middle East is a classic example of not being able to comprehend the root causes of an ongoing conflict. Therefore, no one can fully grasp the issue except God.

The vast majority of a billion Muslims in over 80 countries believe Israel and the Jews are the problem. While many Christians and nations, along with Jews around the world, see the Muslim governments and the Jihadist terrorist organizations as the problem, few understand that God comprehends what is happening. In His timing, He will reveal the answers in ways we will never fully understand.

From Covenant to Eternal Plan

Let's start with what we can understand. God's love for His people prevents Him from remaining silent. His heart is that none should perish. Thus, God does everything possible so that everyone can come to know His plan of salvation. The Bible says He doesn't want even one person to perish.

Nevertheless, the prophet Isaiah brings our Creator's message of consequences for sin, along with a message of eternal hope. When Adam sinned in the Garden of Eden, God brought judgment upon him and Eve. Yet, He also promised to save them and all those who believe in Him throughout the generations from their sin. Faith became the conduit for us to be reconciled with God. The promise of salvation will remain until His plan is finished.

This plan led God to choose a man named Abram, who later would receive a new name, Abraham. As Abraham, he represented God's new vision for the whole world. God promised He would bless him. Through him, our Creator would bless all of the families on earth. Thus, through Abraham's descendant, Jesus, God would reconcile

Himself in love with all who believe in and follow Jesus Christ as their Savior. Jesus's blood seals this covenant.

From Light to Darkness

Through Abraham's descendants, the Hebrews, or as we know them, the Jewish people, Jesus would be born. He is a descendant of their great King David. God began the process through Abraham to teach that there is only one God, and all others were false gods or demons, Satan's followers. The Hebrews were to be His chosen people to teach the nations of the earth who God is and how they could know His love and salvation.

Instead of being a light to the nations by sharing who God is and helping others leave the darkness of their false gods, the Hebrews became corrupted. They began to worship the false gods of other peoples. It was time for them to repent of their wicked ways and return to loving and worshiping the holy God of Abraham.

For thirteen hundred years, God did all He could to train Israel to fulfill His plan, but they had lost their God-ordained vision by Isaiah's time. So, God raised Isaiah to be His prophet, to speak His mind and remind the Hebrews of their reason for existence.

God does not compromise truth. His ways are not our ways, as the Bible teaches. Because of His love and holiness, our Creator is moved to save us from our sins. By worshiping idols and breaking commandments, the Jewish people had fallen away from God. They were in grave danger of eternal death–everlasting separation from

God–because they had forsaken God's vision for their nation and lives.

Isaiah 6:1-8 is a flashback of when the *Lord of Hosts*, Jesus Christ, gave Isaiah a fiery message, commissioning him as a prophet. He saw the Lord seated on a throne. An angelic being cried out, "Holy, holy, holy," as the posts shook and smoke filled the room. Overcome, Isaiah declared himself "undone," confessing his "unclean lips" and acknowledging the sinfulness of his people. A fiery coal from the altar was brought to his lips, purging his sin and preparing him for his calling. Then, when the *Lord of Hosts* asked, "Whom shall I send?" Isaiah replied, "Here am I! Send me." Cleansed and empowered, Isaiah was ready to confront God's people with their sins and call them to repentance.

In Isaiah Chapter One, we first learn God is angry with His people. Through the prophet, He communicates that He will no longer hear their prayers or receive their sacrifices. Their hands are covered in blood from their sins. They lost God's vision of living as holy people and being a light to the nations.

In love, God reasons with them by clearly stating that even though their actions have been grievous, they could repent. Despite all that had happened, it wasn't too late to choose Him as their only God. He promised to wash them clean from their transgressions, to be whiter than snow. If they refused, the *Lord of Hosts* would bring terrible judgment upon them.

The pattern of covenant-breaking with God continued throughout Israel's history. Even after Jesus established

His church by grafting the Gentiles into the Jewish people through faith in Him, the pattern continued.

While in Cuba, I received a divine message, just as Isaiah was called to warn Israel. The warning is not just symbolic—it is a reality the world will soon face.

From Warnings to Fulfillment

Awakened in the middle of the night in Cuba, I received three words from the Spirit: "hurricane of fire." I saw images of the 2025 fires raging in California that had swept through the Palisades and Malibu. The disaster destroyed over 10,000 homes, businesses, schools, and churches. Twenty-nine people lost their lives.

Fueled by up to 100-mile-per-hour winds, dense underbrush, and an inability to stop the intense flames, historic tragedy struck the surrounding beauty of Los Angeles. We, along with the rest of the world, viewed the hurricane of fire on our screens.

Reports spread that the leadership ignored warnings of the potential danger. The Fire Department budget had been cut, leaving fewer firefighters to combat the initial flames. Failure to clear the underbrush enabled that growth to fuel the flames. Water levels in the reservoirs were insufficient to douse the inferno.

Yet, I was told in the Spirit that even more horrific events would one day strike the earth. Nations and individuals were ignoring the warnings given in the Bible by Jesus and His messengers.

John prophesied in Revelation 20 that Jesus will return in His glory as the *Lord of Hosts*, the Commander of God's heavenly armies, to defeat all those in rebellion against His kingdom. He describes the day of eternal judgment when Jesus condemns all who refused to enter into His blood covenant with Him and who persecuted His brethren, the Jews. They, along with Satan and his demons, kings, and their armies, will be cast into a lake of fire.

Peter describes in Second Peter Chapter 3 how many will scoff at the mention of Jesus's return, treating it with disbelief and ridicule. He warned that Jesus would come with a hurricane of fire to consume all that is evil and sinful in this world to create a new heaven and earth, as described in Revelation Chapters 21 and 22.

Jesus, in Matthew Chapters 24 and 25, prophesied the signs of His return and what will happen when our *Lord of Hosts* descends from heaven to judge the nations and individuals for their failure to repent and believe in Him. As the Holy Judge and Creator, Jesus will separate the sheep from the goats. The sheep who follow Him in faith will be rewarded, and the goats who reject Him will be punished.

Just as Los Angeles suffered from the hurricane of fire because they ignored the warnings given, so will those who did not heed the warnings of Jesus and His messengers.

From Invitation to Decision

Today, Jesus has sent messengers to the nations of the earth, to every tribe, tongue, and ethnic group, to call them to follow Him. They are to put away their idols and reject the false teachings of man-made religions and philosophies. As they do so, they will cry out in repentance for their sins to be forgiven and come to Jesus for forgiveness and reconciliation with God. He will embrace them as He has you: in love. Jesus is the only way, truth, and life to an eternal relationship with God.

All those who reject His call and fail to heed His warnings will be consumed by holy fire, so all sin and evil are removed from the earth. Those who trust in Jesus Christ alone will receive an eternal reward far beyond imagination. They will enjoy the blessings of God forever, restored fully to the image of God with resurrected bodies.

This message of love and life is heralded by God's messengers on television, podcasts, social media, movies, books, and in person in every nation. God is reaching out in His love so no one will perish.

Many question how a loving God can bring disasters that cause so much suffering. But Scripture reminds us that He is sovereign over all things—even the calamities we struggle to understand. As the Lord says in Isaiah, *"I form the light and create darkness, I make peace and create calamity; I, the Lord, do all these things.'* (Isaiah 45:7). We may not always see the purpose, but He has never lost control.

What many fail to understand is that Jesus created every person with an eternal soul before they ever received a physical body, beginning in their mother's womb. We are not temporary beings.

When we die, and everyone will die, our souls continue to exist. *"And as it is appointed for men to die once, but after this the judgment*" (Hebrews 9:27). The reality of eternity is not a metaphor—it's a certainty. And it leads us to a sobering truth: to create a perfect paradise without sin or evil, God must separate those who have rejected His sacrifice of love.

Jesus warned of this. *"Depart from Me, you cursed, into the everlasting fire prepared for the devil and his angels"* (Matthew 25:41). The lake of fire, described in Revelation, represents more than punishment—it is the final and complete separation from God. Not because He is unloving, but because He is holy.

As I took these thoughts into my mind, like the prophet Daniel when God gave him visions of the future, I was deeply troubled and unable to sleep. The hurricane of fire is coming soon, but in God's time, not as we measure time. "Do not forget this one thing, that with the Lord one day is as a thousand years, and a thousand years as one day" (2 Peter 3:8). Jesus has been gone for only two days in the Spirit. We have entered the third day, the season of His return. Just as He rose from the dead on the third day, His return is imminent.

Jesus prophesied that when the Gentiles no longer trampled Jerusalem, it would mark the season of His return. In 1967, Israel reestablished Jerusalem as its capital, fulfilling this prophecy. Our Lord said we would then have one generation before He descends from heaven in His glory to fulfill His promises of vengeance against those who persecuted and killed His followers. Nevertheless, a generation is undetermined in the Bible. It can be 40, 70, 100, or even 900 years, like Methuselah's generation. What we can know is that we live in the season of His return and must prepare the world for His Second Coming.

In Matthew 24:44, Jesus tells the world to get their house in order. The day of the Lord will be like Noah's day before the flood. People will go about their business unconcerned about the true purposes of God. During this time, Satan will be concentrating on destroying families. He has penetrated households with his lies and deception via television, the internet, music, books, and false witnesses. Jesus stated there would be false Christs, teachers, and prophets. The man of lawlessness will come to deceive even the elect of God (Second Thessalonians 2:1-12).

The hurricane of fire will come like the Los Angeles fires: a relentless force destroying everything in its path. What we must appreciate is that by grace, our *Lord of Hosts* has given humanity the ability to choose life with Jesus or deny Him and His salvation, leading to eternal fire. Thus, the questions remain:

Will Jesus truly come and send His fire from heaven to consume the armies of Satan and the kings who reject Him? Revelation 20:7-10 declares that God will rain down fire from heaven to devour them.

Do you believe that Jesus will come in His glory from heaven with His angelic army? Is your faith merely an intellectual belief, or is it a Biblical faith that trusts He is coming again? If you believe, it should transform your lifestyle as you prepare for His return.

What choice have you made? By God's grace, humanity can accept Christ's salvation or reject Him. Are you living in faith and preparing for Christ's return, or are you ignoring the reality of His coming judgment?

The day is imminent. As one of His messengers, I call you to repent of your sins and put all your faith in Jesus Christ alone. You cannot serve two masters and escape His judgment. There is only one Lord and Master, and that is Jesus Christ. Give your heart and life fully to Jesus. You will know the love of God and His eternal salvation. As for me and my household, we choose Jesus!

From Then to Now

The call to repent of our evil ways began with one nation, Israel. Now, it applies to all nations. As the return of Jesus draws nearer, Satan knows his time is short. We can see his hand of seduction and evil in the church. Second Thessalonians 2:3 warns of a "falling away" or a mass departure from the Church by believers. It has come in these latter days. The Barna Group's research shows that 64% of those 18 to 29 have left the church. [1] Think about these implications. Not only have young adults left the church in record numbers, but it is safe to assume that many will not return to raise their children in the church. For Christianity as a whole, the Pew Research Center reports a decline in the number of Americans who identify as Christian. [2]

Isaiah's vision concerns not only his lifetime but also the latter days. (Isaiah 2:2-11,12-22) This phrase "latter days" speaks of Jesus as the *Lord of Hosts* who returns to make right all that has fallen into sin and corruption. It is a time for us to separate ourselves from the idols of this world and give ourselves solely to Jesus Christ.

Again, Isaiah's prophetic words apply to us now and in the future. The same language in Isaiah is used in Revelation 6 regarding the opening of the Sixth Seal. Isaiah 2:12 describes the "Day of the Lord" as a time of judgment on hubris and the worshiping of false ideas. Revelation 6:12-17 describes the opening of the Sixth Seal as a moment of judgment, reiterating what Isaiah described.

Yes, these prophetic words can be applied to the history of Judah and Jerusalem, but see how they describe our world today and in the near future. The idolatry the Hebrews adopted is now global, even in churches. While this book is not meant to be a study of the Book of Revelation, it's important to understand that Jesus's seven letters to the churches in Revelation are a prophetic plea to avoid compromise in your beliefs, seek repentance, and prepare as the days may grow darker during our lifetime. There will be a time when God's terror will come upon those who have not repented and surrendered their heart to Jesus.

Secular humanism has spread into almost every culture. It is the philosophy that God does not exist, but that humanity is the center of the universe. We no longer need God. Problems can be solved by our own genius rather than the wisdom of God. This approach is foolish. It's a demonic deception that comes straight from Adam's sin. Now, it proliferates throughout the globe in the guise of religion.

Combined with this heresy is the return of the false gods worshipped by the ancient cultures. Practices such as astrology, crystal healing, and invoking the universe have greatly increased. Search TikTok using the hashtag "astrology," and you'll discover 4.5 million videos. [3] The root of this is the spirit of the Antichrist that redefines Jesus as merely a great prophet instead of God. The goal is to diminish Jesus's divine identity.

The Holy Spirit convicted the church in Ephesus that they had lost their first love for Jesus. Today, many churches have also lost sight of their first love. The time to repent and ask the *Lord of Hosts* to restore your love for Jesus is now.

From Darkness to Light

Jesus calls you to know His gift of eternal life and become His messenger of hope to a dark and self-destructive world. Give Him your heart and life. Turn from your old vision of living and accept His vision for your life, and you will know His eternal love and liberty in living for Him.

The same problem and solution I presented applies to Israel and the Middle East. Sin is the root cause. This sin is the rejection of Jesus as the *Lord of Hosts*, as the Messiah, and only Savior. Israel as a whole still rejects Jesus, as do the Muslim cultures. Therefore, they fail to have God's vision for their personal lives and nations.

The Jews, for the most part, understand God's vision through Abraham and the covenant God made with him. The land of Israel is their God-promised right. They love God but do not accept Jesus Christ. The solution is that, in the end, God will make it clear to every Jew that Jesus is the Messiah. God will fulfill His covenant with the descendants of Abraham. They will "see their Deliverer come out of Zion" (Isaiah 59:20, Romans 11:26) and believe in Jesus as their King and *Lord of Hosts*.

Jesus will come from heaven to rescue them from the nations that seek to wipe them from the face of the earth. All the armies of Satan and the kings will be destroyed. Our Lord will reign in Jerusalem over all the nations of the earth. He will create a new heaven and earth with the Jewish people in the lead of that reign.

Just as I found purpose and hope through God's grace, I saw His hand in restoring Israel and His ultimate plan for humanity. Throughout history, the Jewish people have faced relentless persecution by nations and empires. They have often been unjustly targeted because of their identity and faith. The atrocities committed against the Jews, including the Holocaust, during which six million were brutally murdered, were acts of human evil, not divine will. Yet, in a profound demonstration of God's sovereignty, even this darkest moment was followed by the rebirth of the nation of Israel, fulfilling biblical prophecy and showing how God can bring restoration and hope out of human tragedy.

Nevertheless, like all people, the Hebrews have a sin nature, but their covenant with God placed them in a unique role to reveal His truth and prepare the way for the Messiah. Their history reflects both the consequences of sin and God's faithfulness in preserving His chosen people.

Their immense suffering, dating from Isaiah's time to the return of the *Lord of Hosts*, is part of God's plan to address humanity's sinfulness and bring people back into a relationship with Him.

From Division to Unity

Now, much of the Muslim world wants to wipe out Israel. Even the United Nations, which played a pivotal role in the establishment of the country of Israel, has betrayed it. On March 24, 2024, the U.N. Security Council called for a resolution demanding an immediate ceasefire in Gaza. Still, it did not guarantee the unconditional release of the Jewish hostages kidnapped during the October 7 attack on Israel by Hamas. The U.S. departed from its tradition of vetoing resolutions harmful to Israel and abstained from the vote. [4]

The escalation of countries turning away from Israel is a grave reminder of the prophecy in Zechariah 12:3: "And it shall happen in that day that I will make Jerusalem a very heavy stone for all peoples." The verse prophesies a time when standing with Israel will become increasingly contentious and burdensome for nations, fulfilling biblical warnings of global opposition.

Events like the October 7, 2023 attack remind us of the spiritual battle that rages globally. Yet, these events also reaffirm the truth of God's Word—that He will never abandon His people or promises. This is a call for believers to use the greatest weapons at our disposal–to intercede in prayer and live as examples of God's love and justice.

I experienced a powerful example when, in May 2024, I attended the Eighth Annual Jerusalem Prayer Breakfast. The event originated in Jerusalem and has since spread around the world. It's a fantastic opportunity for world leaders to pray for Israel, other countries, and Jews worldwide. We also gather to fulfill God's vision for Israel and the world. This vision was first revealed in Genesis 12, which states that through Abraham's Seed, God would redeem humanity and nations through the Messiah, Jesus Christ.

When we met in the chambers of the Knesset–Israel's Parliament–and later at our conference meetings, I perceived from listening to the Jewish leaders and other speakers that their hearts were broken. They had not recovered from suffering the unimaginable terrors of a demonic attack brought forth by Hamas terrorists. To make matters worse, they could not understand why the world had condemned Israel. The isolation and rejection they felt from the lack of support contributed to their pain and confusion.

On the last night of our meeting, I was humbled to address the attendees, Jews and Christians alike. I shared with them the message that the Messiah of Isaiah 61, who loves justice, heals the brokenhearted, and consoles those "who mourn in Zion," is the Jesus mentioned in Luke 4 who fulfilled Scripture. The *Lord of Hosts* is healing broken hearts and "proclaiming liberty" in the midst of their agonizing war.

From Hopeless to Hope

Just as I found purpose and hope through God's grace, I see His hand at work in restoring Israel and His ultimate plan for humanity. My journey mirrors God's promise of redemption for individuals and nations alike.

Even though the Jews broke their covenant with God, He promised in Jeremiah 31:31 that when God regathered the Jews to the newly reborn nation of Israel, they would never cease to be a nation again. However, it would appear that in the latter days, they would be surrounded, and their survival would look hopeless. But there is hope. Jesus will come to save them and restore Israel as the leader of the nations, with Jesus as the King of all. Although the world seems to grow darker, God's promise shines brighter. The message isn't just about Israel or the Middle East—it's a call for us to align our lives with God's vision and share His love with a hurting world.

Out of Judgment, God always brings hope. Jesus is the hope of glory. God never fails to fulfill His promises and prophecy. "Never again" is the cry of the Jews declaring the prophecies of God that Israel will not fall to the plan of Satan and the Gentile nations but be resurrected to eternal life as Jesus rose from the grave to show the world He is Lord.

GOING DEEPER | Chapter 2

Reflect and Respond

1. Describe a personal experience that deepened your faith. If you have not yet experienced one, how can you seek to experience God more fully?

2. Describe a time you placed your identity in something temporary. What happened when that thing was taken away, or didn't fulfill you?

3. When Isaiah saw the Lord, he immediately recognized his sinfulness, and a burning coal purified his lips (Isaiah 6:5-7). The author also describes feeling completely cleansed in Jesus's presence. What does this tell us about God's forgiveness and our need for purification?

4. The Jewish people were called to be a light to the nations, but instead, they lost sight of their mission and began worshiping false gods (Isaiah 1). In today's world, what are some of the modern-day "idols" that can distract believers from their purpose? How can you ensure that your focus remains on Christ alone?

For Further Study & Reflection

1. Isaiah answered God's call with, "Here am I! Send me." (Isaiah 6:8) Describe what answering God's call looks like in your life. Are you resisting or embracing His plan?

2. The "Hurricane of Fire" described in the chapter warns of coming judgment, just as Jesus spoke of in Matthew 24-25, and as John wrote in Revelation 20. Many ignored the 2025 California wildfires' warnings, just as people ignore spiritual warnings. How can you help others recognize the urgency of following Christ?

3. In 2 Peter 3, Peter warns that many will scoff at the idea of Jesus's return, yet he reminds believers that "with the Lord, a day is like a thousand years" (2 Peter 3:8-10). The author connects this passage to our present time, saying we are in the "third day." How does viewing time from God's perspective change how we live? What does it mean to be spiritually prepared for Jesus' return?

4. God repeatedly called Israel to repentance and offered restoration. How does this reflect His character? What steps can you take to ensure you align with His will?

5. Jesus warned that in the last days, many would be deceived by false teachings (Matthew 24:24). The chapter describes the rise of secular humanism, astrology, and other false beliefs. Why do you think people are drawn to these alternative spiritualities? How can believers discern truth from deception and help others do the same?

6. The world appears to be growing darker, yet God promises to bring hope. List specific actions you can do to reflect Christ's love. Choose one or two to put into action in the week ahead.

7. The author affirms Joshua 24:15: "As for me and my household, we will serve the Lord." In a world where faith is declining and many are turning away from God (2 Thessalonians 2:3), what steps can you take to ensure your faith remains strong?

Denial blinds both nations and individuals. The warnings have been given—through prophets, history, and the voice of God Himself. The question is not whether judgment will come, but whether we will wake up before it does.

3

The Judgment

Throughout history, the human race has mastered countless strategies for survival, yet denial—a force that has fueled wars, natural disasters, and personal destruction—remains one of our greatest weaknesses. We excel at ignoring the reality of our desolation, of being disconnected from the purpose God has intended for us.

The recent wildfires in Los Angeles serve as a haunting example. Every year, firefighters and environmental experts warn about the dry conditions, urging proactive measures to prevent catastrophe. Yet, despite repeated warnings, many ignore the danger, believing that disaster won't strike them. Then, when the winds shift, the flames engulf neighborhoods, leaving behind only ashes and regret. The signs were there all along, but people failed to act.

This pattern of denial extends far beyond wildfires. It can be seen in wars that could have been prevented, civilizations that ignored their decay, and individuals who refused to acknowledge their need for redemption.

- Before World War II, world leaders dismissed Hitler's ambitions, believing he could be reasoned with. Their refusal to confront evil led to the deaths of over 60 million people.
- The Roman Empire, once a symbol of strength, crumbled under moral decay and corruption, blind to the cracks forming within its foundation.
- The captain of the "unsinkable" Titanic ignored multiple iceberg warnings, leading to one of the worst maritime disasters in history.

Denial is not just a historical failing; it is a spiritual one. The people of Isaiah's day refused to believe that their idolatry and disobedience would bring consequences. They assumed that because they were God's chosen people, judgment would never come. But history, both ancient and modern, shows that ignoring warnings leads to destruction—whether in cities, nations, or souls.

Like the Hebrews of Isaiah's time, we, too, live in an age where warnings go unheard. We dismiss the consequences of moral decline, spiritual rebellion, and rejecting God's truth. But just as judgment came to ancient Israel, it will come again. The question is: Will we listen before it's too late?

God's Path

The Jews in Isaiah's day denied their rejection of God. When worshiping false gods, they willingly blinded themselves to their betrayal. Even worse, they took the Covenant for granted and refused to believe God would bring judgment against them. Yet, judgment was necessary to restore them to whole-hearted devotion.

They could not conceive that God would allow the Assyrian army to destroy Israel and then ravage Judea and threaten Jerusalem with destruction. Despite numerous warnings from prophets like Isaiah, they wouldn't believe the prophetic words but chose to trust in false prophets and ungodly leaders.

The kings and prophets rationalized that they were God's chosen people through whom the world's salvation would come. Surely, God would never allow them to be removed as a nation or be taken captive.

Denial leads to death and desolation. We see this in the increase in addictions, broken marriages, failed businesses, and misguided nations. Since secular humanism has convinced people that there is no God, judgment is nonexistent. Or worse, many followers of Jesus don't believe that a loving God could condemn sinners to hell.

For one, they do not believe there is a hell–eternal separation from God. Or, if it exists, it wouldn't apply to them. After all, isn't hell for the most evil people? Yet, Jesus spoke clearly about its reality and warned of eternal judgment.

The road to everlasting separation from God is wide, and the path to God and eternal life is narrow. This is why we must understand that Jesus Christ, the *Lord of Hosts*, commands all power in heaven's armies. He will return to judge those who have not repented, both living and dead (2 Timothy 4:1). His actions will be in holiness and power, carrying out judgment with perfect justice. Those who haven't turned to Him will face the consequences of their rejection, not because He is unloving, but because He is holy, set apart in righteousness and utterly opposed to sin.

God's Judgments

Isaiah explains what this judgment means and how God works to redeem people and nations.

First, God raises up a messenger to call people to repent of their idolatry, false beliefs, and sinful lifestyles. If they do not turn from their ways of living and continue to fail to trust in God alone, He will bring judgment, as the messenger warned.

It's what I call "temporary judgment" in this life. In Isaiah's day, God allowed the Assyrian army to bring judgment upon the northern tribes of Israel and Judah. They refused to stop trusting in false gods and looked to the army of Egypt to save them from the Assyrians—a bad move!

God would have stopped the consequences if they had completely given their hearts to the *Lord of Hosts.* He had done so before through King Hezekiah and Isaiah. These two men led the people to repentance and trust in God for their deliverance from the Assyrian army. God miraculously saved Jerusalem from destruction. He then sent the Angel of Death in the night to destroy the Assyrian army. Their king fled home, where his sons murdered him.

It's serious business when God calls people to trust in Him for salvation. Isaiah said God would spare a remnant who repented and relied on His promise to Abraham and David. Through their Seed, Jesus Christ, He would bring salvation to the Jews and all nations.

The other judgment is eternal for those people and nations who never repent and refuse to trust in Jesus Christ alone. Isaiah describes this as eternal separation from God (Isaiah 66:24). They will never experience the coming age, the millennial kingdom of the Messiah.

Jesus describes this eternal judgment in Matthew 25:31-46, where He returns in glory, separates the righteous from the wicked, and says to those who rejected Him, "Depart from Me, you cursed, into the everlasting fire prepared for the devil and his angels."

Revelation Chapters 14-20 further expand on the final destiny of those not found in the Book of Life. As the Commander of the Heavenly Armies, Jesus is the author of God's judgment. Those who have chosen to be Christ-followers are exempt. Those who didn't choose Christ will be separated from the presence of God and His kingdom forever. They will face the most unimaginable fate: eternal torment in the fires of hell, enduring unending pain and separation from God's love and redemption.

God's Consistent Call

Denial has shaped history, leading to destruction and suffering. Yet, it is not only nations that fall into this trap—individuals, too, often refuse to acknowledge their desolation, their separation from the purpose God has intended. But Jesus is still calling the world to awaken.

Isaiah called Israel to repentance; Jesus warned of eternal judgment. And God is still calling people today. In one small church in Pakistan, after I preached the message of Jesus' return and the urgency of repentance, several individuals received the same vision—Jesus speaking to them, calling them to surrender to Him. The burdens of false religion, oppressive governments, and spiritual despair had weighed them down. But in that moment, they saw the truth: they did not have to remain in darkness. His hand was reaching out, offering them hope and redemption.

Just as Isaiah's audience had a choice—to turn back to God or remain in denial—so do we. Many today are weary of traditions that enslave them, longing for something real. Jesus' invitation remains:

"Come to Me… and I will give you rest" (Matthew 11:28). Throughout Scripture, judgment is never the final word. Justice follows—God sets things right according to His holiness. But before judgment and justice, His mercy calls, giving us the chance to turn back to Him. The question is, will we listen?

Even today, this judgment is not limited to individuals; it extends to nations and groups that oppose God's will and covenant promises. Scripture affirms that those who act against God's chosen people will face His wrath. As stated in Joel 3:2, God declares He will enter into judgment with the nations on behalf of Israel. The threats posed by Iran, Hezbollah, and Hamas are not merely geopolitical conflicts but reflections of the spiritual battle described in Scripture. Nations rise against God's chosen people, yet He remains sovereign. These events remind us of the ongoing struggle between good and evil and the assurance that the *Lord of Hosts* will bring ultimate justice.

In Isaiah's visions, the *Lord of Hosts* brings temporary consequences upon Israel, Judah, Jerusalem, and the nations surrounding Israel. Similarly, in Revelation, Jesus brings judgment on a global scale against Babylon, Satan, rebellious kings and armies, all who refuse to repent and acknowledge Him as Lord and Savior. In this context, *Babylon* symbolizes the world system opposed to God, marked by spiritual corruption, idolatry, and rebellion. This judgment ultimately becomes eternal.

God's offer of hope precedes this judgment, as seen in Isaiah 1:18: "Come now, and let us reason together. Isaiah 2:2-4 speaks of a future where nations seek the Lord. God's heart is to bring His people to repentance so they can trust in Him alone. Revelation 14 represents this truth in action. "Fear God and give glory to Him, for the hour of His judgment has come..." (Revelation 14:7). It is a timeless Biblical principle found not just in Isaiah and Revelation but throughout the Bible. God consistently calls for humanity to turn to Him before His justice is administered.

In the latter days, Jesus promises to save Israel. Ezekiel Chapters 38 and 39 declare that God will deliver Israel from the armies He has caused to come against them. This will lead to Jesus's return and fulfill God's covenant with Abraham. All nations will know that the God of Israel is the only true God. His name will be glorified among all nations, including Israel.

Revelation 14 precedes the *Lord of Hosts'* judgment on Babylon, Satan, and all who refuse to repent of their idolatry. It begins by depicting Jesus as the Lamb of God with 144,000 "who have his Father's name written on their forehead." They are His complete holy messengers who trust in Him alone.

Then, three angels or heavenly messengers proclaim the Lamb's warning, born out of His love for all people—the One who died for every nation, tribe, and tongue. The first angel announces the everlasting Gospel, calling everyone to fear God and give Him glory, for the hour of judgment has come. The message is clear: worship the Lord God alone. The second angel gives testimony to the counterfeit way of Satan and the world. Babylon has fallen. It cannot save you.

The third angel warns that anyone who worships the beast will suffer the terrible judgment of the *Lord of Hosts*. The choice is obvious. Flee evil and idolatry to save yourself or suffer the torment of eternal separation from the God who loves you. Those who listen are the saints of God who will know His peace and rest for eternity. They are the redeemed of the Lamb. Then, Revelation Chapter 14 closes with the Son of Man coming in His glory to bring the harvest of judgment and the grapes of His wrath.

God Dismissed

In Revelation Chapter 18, Jesus, as the *Lord of Hosts*, causes the world system of Babylon to fall. In Revelation Chapter 19, He returns to earth not as the Lamb of

God but as the mighty warrior, the *Lord of Hosts*. He's accompanied by the resurrected saints and His army of angels. He defeats Satan, the beast, the false prophets, and the kings and their armies.

At the White Throne of Judgment, Jesus finishes His acts of justice by condemning all who have rejected Him and rebelled against God in their attempt to establish the kingdom of Satan. They are cast into the lake of fire. After this judgment, Jesus will make all things new, heaven and earth, with a new Jerusalem. Paradise will be restored in the glorious eternal presence of the Father and Son.

Many dismiss this concept of God and Jesus as cruel and unloving. A loving God could never do this. If our Creator is all-powerful, why does He not act to stop all of humanity's suffering? God responds that He has. God became Man in Jesus Christ to take our sins and death upon Himself so we could be reconciled to God and enjoy His intimacy forever.

Our concept of time has one dimension; while God is not contained by time, He transcends it. What we perceive as eons are days to Him; figuratively speaking, a thousand years is but a day. In God's time, Jesus has only been gone for two days. Time has no bearing on Him. His actions supersede time; we, on the other hand, are subject to the dominion of time.

Many question God's nature because we are aware of the evil and pain that have persisted over centuries. To God, our history is merely an instant. Thus, He acts swiftly to save us from our corruption and wickedness. Our *Lord of*

Hosts enters into our suffering to take on our sins because of His love for us. In Jesus Christ, we have a personal God we can love and follow.

Those who have never experienced this God cannot conceive what I have just stated. However, once a person experiences God's love, it becomes their anchor throughout life to endure trials and tribulations. Our hope in Him is a certainty, not a maybe. I can endure "all things through Christ who strengthens me" (Philippians 4:13).

God's Last Resort

Through Isaiah, God warns us of the eternal dangers of seeking after other gods and refusing to humble ourselves to confess our sins. Jesus calls us to total dependence on God, as His truth states that we can do nothing to save ourselves from our transgressions. Jesus alone has paid the price for our wickedness, as we "all have sinned and fall short of the glory of God" (Romans 3:23).

Judgment is God's last resort in dealing with humanity's rebellion. Everything He does beforehand is an invitation to return to Him in complete love and devotion. Jesus is the gate to forgiveness and reconciliation. Through His sinless life and sacrificial death on the cross, He is the bridge to cross over from death to life. God promises to deliver us from our sinful rebellion.

Our destiny is to be restored fully to the image of God that was corrupted by our sin. Jesus says, "I am the way, the truth, and the life" (John 14:6). To prove this, He raised His friend Lazarus from the dead, foreshadowing that He would die for our sins. Jesus rose on the third day as the one sign humanity can never duplicate, proving He alone is God. Jesus is the anointed Savior for all who repent and believe in Him.

Isaiah makes it clear that God is long-suffering with the Jews' rebellion and idolatry. In the end, His plan of salvation will happen. The sins of humanity and the deception of Satan had no power to stop God's vision of using the Jews to be the chosen people to bring forth the Savior into the world. The *Lord of Hosts* will be a Jew, the Seed of Abraham, the descendant of King David, and "the Lamb of God who takes away the sin of the world. His name will be Jesus, Immanuel, God with us, the Christ" (John 1:29).

God's Touch

Because God's way of salvation is decreed by His nature of love and holiness, all human rebellion must be eradicated from His eternal kingdom. All evil, including Satan and his demons, must be excluded from the Holy Realm.

Like a master computer program, Jesus will wipe out all the corrupted software resulting from sin. In an instant, the *Lord of Hosts* will enter the new software of a holy and loving creation. With one touch of the keyboard, everything will become new. Yet, we can't even imagine a perfect world where we are in love with God, self, and one another.

Our corrupt nature will be removed. We will no longer act out of selfishness or pride. Our lusts will be no more.

We will love as God loves and act as Jesus acted to please, honor, and obey His Father. Paradise lost will be no more. We will know a whole new way of life in love and oneness in the glory of God.

We will never have a bad thought. Never utter an evil word or hurt another human being. No action of humanity or science can bring this about. Humanity has tried countless times to create a world free from oppression and inequality, only to create worse monsters who murder the hearts and souls of all those who oppose them. Only Jesus, as the *Lord of Hosts*, can create a new world of peace and justice for all.

That is why in Isaiah 9, the only answer for our salvation is the child who is also the Mighty God, the Prince of Peace, and the Everlasting Father. No mere mortal can do what Isaiah describes. He will rule with everlasting justice and harmony with all of creation. The lion lies down with the lamb. Nations have no more wars. Jesus reigns over a world transformed by the word of His mouth.

Just as Jesus spoke creation into existence, He will do once more for all eternity for everyone who has been born again of the Spirit. His offer of this free gift of salvation is open to all people. In the end, every knee will bow, and every tongue will confess He is Lord.

Evil is like radioactive waste. If left out amongst us, it will infect and kill all who are exposed. God must cleanse the earth of all evil to bring in a new heaven and earth. One that is pure and holy, reflecting His image of love and righteousness. This is the call of the *Lord of Hosts*, as He died to set us free from sin and death to prepare us for a new world. He must lead the heavenly hosts in removing all vestiges of evil to end this age of corruption and wickedness.

Trust in Jesus alone is the message in the later chapters of Isaiah. An unbeatable army from Assyria surrounds Jerusalem. The Hebrews are tempted to look back to Egypt to save them. They do not understand that God is creating a situation in which Jerusalem is alone. Egypt cannot save them. The *Lord of Hosts* is the sole hope of survival. In what ways are you figuratively looking to Egypt instead of looking to God?

God's Invitation

Can you see what I've described in Chapter 1 about the situation with the modern state of Israel? It stands alone, fighting armies on all sides, with Iran as the major enemy. Israel is tempted to look to the U.S. for salvation, but God says, trust in Me.

Isaiah tells Jerusalem that the *Lord of Hosts* will remove their blindness so the Hebrews can see that their Deliverer is God and Him alone. The Apostle Paul, in Romans 11, writes that one day, Israel will see the Deliverer come out of Zion, and all Israel will be saved by recognizing Jesus as the Messiah.

Denial closes our eyes to history's warnings and God's truth. Just as the Hebrews trusted in false gods and Egypt and the world dismissed Hitler's rise to power, we too often look to our imperfect solutions rather than to the

Savior. The tendency to deny truth is rooted in our sin nature, which resists surrender and longs to remain in control. As the *Lord of Hosts*, Jesus calls us to trust in Him alone, reminding us that His judgment is always paired with an invitation to eternal grace.

GOING DEEPER | Chapter 3

Reflect & Respond

1. Read Isaiah 6:1-5. Isaiah's warnings about God's judgment came from the *Lord of Hosts,* a title that emphasizes Jesus's authority over nations and armies. How does Isaiah 6:1-5 reveal the majesty and authority of the *Lord of Hosts*? How should this understanding of God impact how we live and trust Him?

2. In Isaiah's time, the people of Israel refused to believe that the *Lord of Hosts* would allow judgment to come upon them. They assumed their status as God's chosen people would protect them, even when they worshiped false gods. How does Isaiah 1:10-15 challenge those who take God's grace for granted?

3. The chapter describes the *Lord of Hosts* as the commander of the heavenly armies who will execute final judgment on the nations. How does this portrayal of Jesus differ from how He is often depicted today? Why is it important to understand both His mercy and His righteous judgment?

4. Throughout Scripture, Egypt often symbolizes reliance on worldly systems rather than trust in God. In what ways are you figuratively looking to Egypt, placing your trust in human wisdom, worldly security, or personal strength, rather than fully relying on the *Lord of Hosts*?

For Further Study & Reflection

1. Read Isaiah 31:1. How does the verse describe the author's point about nations rejecting God and trusting in their strengths and alliances for security? What are some modern-day examples of misplaced trust?

2. Read Isaiah 10:20-22. Though judgment came, the *Lord of Hosts* preserved a faithful remnant through whom He would fulfill His covenant. How does this theme of judgment and restoration reflect God's character? What encouragement can you draw from this truth when facing difficult times?

3. Read Revelation 14:6-7. How does this show God's desire to save rather than condemn?

4. The phrase The *Lord of Hosts* appears over 200 times in the Bible, emphasizing Jesus's sovereign rule over heaven and earth. Why do you think God revealed Himself to Isaiah with this title? How does knowing Jesus as the *Lord of Hosts* deepen your faith and change how you pray?

5. Read Romans 11. The Apostle Paul writes that one day, Israel will see the Deliverer come out of Zion and all of Israel will be saved by recognizing Jesus as the Messiah. What does Paul's message in Romans 11 teach about God's mercy toward both Jews and Gentiles? How does this shape how you view salvation and God's ultimate plan for humanity?

6. Continue reflecting and praying about how your faith should be in the *Lord of Hosts* rather than worldly systems.

May your prayer echo Revelation 22:20.

> "Come, Lord Jesus, come!"
>
> Grant me the gift of brokenness before You. Forgive me of all of my idolatry and pride and lusts. Restore me to oneness with You. May I experience the love and faithfulness of Your intimacy. Use me for Your glory.

7. Read Isaiah 37:33-36. What does this story teach you about spiritual warfare and the power of God to fight for His people? How does this apply to challenges in your own life?

While many resist God's warnings, He continues to call individuals such as Isaiah and Moses to rise up and follow His will. Each encounter with God as the *Lord of Hosts* becomes a moment of transformation, reshaping lives, and altering the course of history.

4

The Encounters

The hot desert wind carried the faint scent of dust and dried grasses, stirring Moses's memories of hunting lions with the young prince of Egypt. The same scorching winds accompanied the thrill of the hunt. His days in the palace of Ramses seemed like an eternity ago. But his new life as a shepherd in Midian was peaceful. His wife, Zipporah, blessed him with love and children. Moses was content living in the household of his father-in-law, Jethro. He had put his past life behind him.

After killing a man to defend his Hebrew people and then fleeing Egypt, Moses settled into a season of blessing. Still, the slavery of the Hebrews in Egypt weighed on his conscience, a burden he couldn't shake despite how much time had passed.

A bewildering sight pulled Moses from his reverie. He walked toward it and realized it was a burning bush. Then, to his astonishment, he saw that the bush wasn't being consumed. How could this be, he wondered? As he continued to watch, he observed an image inside the flame. Was it an angel?

Then the voice of God spoke, “Moses, Moses!”

“Here I am,” the puzzled shepherd replied.

Moses was about to have his first encounter with the God of Abraham, Isaac, and Jacob. He was on holy ground and overwhelmed. “Moses hid his face, for he was afraid to look upon God.” (Exodus 3:6).

God knew what Moses saw when he lived in Egypt: the oppression of the Hebrews. He had heard their pleas to be rescued from the harsh conditions they were forced to endure. God planned to save them and bring them freedom and abundance “to a land flowing with milk and honey” (Exodus 3:8).

Moses must have been tracking with God up to this point. And then God makes the big reveal: Moses, I’ve picked you to bring my people out of bondage, out of Egypt.

Now, Moses is even more bewildered than when he observed the burning bush. "Who am I that I should go to Pharaoh and that I should bring the children of Israel out of Egypt?" Moses had more questions. How would he answer when the Hebrews asked what God’s name is? “And God said to Moses, 'I AM WHO I AM.' Thus you shall say to the children of Israel, 'I AM has sent me to you.'" (Exodus 3:5-14)

Holiness Revealed

Encounters with God are recorded throughout the Bible, from Adam to Cain to Noah to Abraham to Moses to David. Isaiah's encounter with God is similar yet different from Moses's.

In Isaiah Chapter 6, we enter the holiness of the temple where the *Lord of Hosts* dwells with

Both men met Jesus as God. Moses met the great I AM. Furthermore, the Gospel of John tells us that Jesus is the great I AM.

- I AM the bread of life. (John 6:35)
- I AM the light of the world. (John 8:12)
- I AM the gate. (John 10:9)
- I AM the Good Shepherd. (John 10:11)
- I AM the resurrection and the life. (John 11:25)
- I AM the way, the truth, and the life. (John 14:6)
- I AM the True Vine. (John 15:1)

Seven times, Jesus is revealed as the I AM, the same name God used in Exodus.

Moses and Isaiah both answer God's call in the same way: "Here I am." The two are reminded of their need for humility and brokenness. Their lives need to be cleansed to be holy. Moses is told to remove his sandals as he is on holy ground in the presence of God. Isaiah has his sin removed by the seraphim, who took the burning coal from the altar and placed it on his lips.

Another similarity is that both are given a mission from Jesus to set His people free. The Hebrews, through Moses, will be delivered from slavery to the Promised Land. Through Isaiah, they will be redeemed from unholy living and are to trust in the *Lord of Hosts* alone as their Savior. They are delivered from the unbeatable Assyrian army as the Angel of Death is sent by God to destroy the soldiers and the king.

In both encounters, God's holiness and power are revealed, yet the context and timing of His appearance differ. While Moses is called during a season of personal peace, Isaiah is called in a moment of national crisis and uncertainty, underscoring the ever-present sovereignty of the *Lord of Hosts*.

As you may recall, the King of Judah has died. Isaiah went into the temple to seek God's guidance and pray for protection for Jerusalem against the Assyrian army. With his leader no longer alive at this key moment in history, Isaiah must feel helpless and hopeless. Then, without warning, God's glory fills the temple. The *Lord of Hosts*, the pre-incarnate Jesus, reminds Isaiah that the true King of Israel is still alive and all-powerful.

Two seraphim, angelic beings, cry out, "Holy, holy, holy, the whole earth is full of His glory!" (Isaiah 6:3). Their words shake the temple's very foundation as God's glory fills the building.

The gift of brokenness is released upon Isaiah as he realizes that he, an unclean man, is in the presence of the most Holy God. This man of vision has a vision of the *Lord of Hosts*. He has seen the true King of Israel.

"Woe is me," he cries out, "for I am undone." The holiness of Jesus and His glory demonstrated to Isaiah that he is a sinful man who needs salvation. He has come to intercede for his people, but realizes he needs cleansing from his unholy ways. "Because I am a man of unclean lips, and I dwell in the midst of a people of unclean lips." (Isaiah 6:5) The apostle John affirms that Isaiah was seeing the glory of Jesus Himself, writing, "These things Isaiah said when he saw His glory and spoke of Him" (John 12:41).

Remember, Jerusalem is full of corruption. The people pay God lip service but don't worship Him as He should be worshiped. They "honor me with their lips, but their hearts are far from Me" (Isaiah 29:13). Isaiah knew the sin of idolatry and perversion that existed with the priests in the temple. Perhaps he is even part of it. The conviction of God crushed his inner being. However, brokenness, complete humility, is a state of utter dependence upon God's mercy and grace.

Potential Realized

Like Isaiah, we must be broken to be made new. The conviction of the Holy Spirit helps us recognize our need for forgiveness and cleansing. The work of the *Lord of Hosts*, Jesus Christ, makes us whole and pure. God answers when we have a profound sense of desperation that moves us to cry out and seek forgiveness from the core of our being. We can't help but be drawn into intimacy and experience love and oneness with our Creator.

Just as there are similarities between Isaiah's and Moses's experiences, there are parallels between Isaiah and

Peter. Of the many encounters recorded in the Gospels, one of my favorites is how Peter first received the gift of brokenness. It happens along the shores of Galilee.

Peter's brother Andrew was one of John the Baptist's disciples. When he heard John call Jesus the "Lamb of God," Andrew was immediately drawn to Him. After spending some time with Jesus, Andrew knew he was in the presence of the Messiah. He could barely contain his excitement and shared his discovery with his older brother.

Andrew brought his brother to Jesus, who said, "You are Simon, the son of Jonah. You shall be called Cephas." From then on, Simon was known as Cephas, Aramaic for Peter (John 1:42).

Jesus told Peter that if he followed Him, He would bring out Peter's God potential—his unique purpose and impact—so that he would no longer be a fisherman but a fisher of men. *"I will use your life to transform the world"*—quite a statement to a man who lived in an insignificant village in the middle of nowhere.

For Simon to grasp his *God potential* and become Peter, his old self had to be broken. So Jesus used Peter's boat as a stage to teach the people along the shoreline. Once Jesus was done, He told the fisherman to take his boat into the deep water and let down his nets (Luke 5:4). But the fisherman had already worked all night and caught nothing. Despite his reluctance, Peter did as Jesus asked. Imagine his surprise when he caught so many fish that the nets were breaking.

The wonder so moved Peter that he fell at Jesus's feet, saying, "Depart from me, for I am a sinful man, O Lord!" (Luke 5:8). He experienced Jesus's glory, and his inner being was broken. He saw himself as a sinner in need of Jesus's forgiveness and salvation. Peter is now ready to start his new life of growing toward being the leader Jesus promised him he would be.

Like Isaiah, who was forever changed by his encounter with the *Lord of Hosts* in the temple, Peter, too, stood face to face with the same holy and sovereign God. Peter did not fully grasp it at the time, but he had just been drafted into the greatest mission ever launched on earth, led by the Commander of heaven's armies. Though his courage would be tested, the trajectory of his life was forever altered. He would go on to help establish the early Church, built on the rock of Christ and the truth of who He is. The God-given potential within him began to unfold.

The parallel between Isaiah's response and Peter's calling reminds us that lives are forever changed when God speaks. When Isaiah answered, "Here I am, send me," it foreshadowed Jesus's call to Peter and the rest of His apostles. This same call has been heard by countless others touched by Jesus in the last 2000 years.

Mission Confirmed

Go is such a short word, but it has an immense Scriptural meaning. All through the Bible, God tells His anointed ones to *go*. Abram, *go* to the land I show you. Moses, *go* to Egypt to rescue My people. Jesus, *go* from Your throne in heaven to save the people. Apostles, *go* into all the world to make followers of Me. To each of us in this day, at this time, *go* and prepare the way for My return.

One of my favorite stories concerning *go* is recorded in *Chasing the Dragon*. God calls a young English woman, Jackie Pullinger, to the mission field. It was the 1960s, and the Vietnam War was escalating. No mission society was willing to send an unmarried woman into the field alone.

Each time Jackie applied, she was refused. Frustrated and puzzled, Jackie met a pastor who advised her to *go*. She wanted the details of how and where, but he simply counseled her to *go*.

Jackie listened and purchased an ocean liner ticket. The voyage would take her to major ports around the world. She prayed when she arrived at each destination: "Is this where I am to *go*?" It wasn't until she arrived in Hong Kong that she knew she was where God had sent her.

When she attempted to disembark, the ship's clerk refused to let her leave. Hong Kong was where the soldiers fighting in Vietnam went for rest from the ravages of war. The clerk assumed Jackie was a prostitute because there could be no other reason why a single woman would want to leave the ship.

Jackie shared her story with the clerk, who asked if she had any family in Hong Kong. She had an uncle, and, despite all odds, the clerk knew him. Jackie was permitted to leave the ship, but still didn't know the details. Where in such a large city should she begin to minister?

After wandering through the streets, she entered a dark place where gangs, prostitutes, and drug dealers reigned.

The place was so full of evil that the city had cut off the power and water, making it even more desolate–a place where desperation thrived.

Yet, it is where God sent her. Despite the dangers she faced, she began to minister, but without much success. After months of failure, she was baptized in the Holy Spirit, and the windows of heaven opened to her. Gang leaders chose to follow Jesus. Prostitutes were set free. Drug addicts were delivered, never to use again. The den of demons Jackie entered was transformed into a sanctuary honoring Jesus.

God has a purpose and plan if you yield your life to Him and decide to be all in for Jesus. As the *Lord of Hosts*, Jesus did battle for Isaiah. Jesus also leads the armies of heaven for you and me, like He did for Jackie.

Calling Heard

Keep in mind how the *Lord of Hosts* responded to Isaiah's consecration–when he was cleansed of sin by the burning coal–with a command: "*Go* and tell this people..." In this moment, Isaiah is entrusted with a message from God that resounds throughout Scripture. This same message is paraphrased in John 12:40, applying it to the people of His time. Yet, both instances reveal a tragic reality: the inability of the Jews in Isaiah's day and in Jesus's day to hear the message of God's salvation. They don't repent because their hearts are closed to God's word.

Even the religious leaders who encountered Jesus were so indoctrinated in false teachings and full of pride that they failed to recognize Jesus for who He is. The *Lord of Hosts* pronounces woes upon them, just as Isaiah did with those in his day who had fallen into sinful lifestyles.

Woes in Scripture indicate lamenting and the consequences of rejecting God's ways. Woe is a word connecting sin and rebellion. In Matthew 23, Jesus uses the term seven times to indicate the hypocrisy of the Pharisees and teachers of the law. In Revelation, woes are pronounced in the last days upon those who reject Jesus. We live in the last days before the coming of Jesus. One indication is that many who profess to follow Jesus have lost their first love for our Lord.

Today, false religions, secular humanism, demonic strongholds, and flawed teachings, even in the church, bring darkness. Jesus has been redefined to rationalize sinful ways. His message of grace and forgiveness is used to rationalize ongoing sin. Scripture is reinterpreted or cherry-picked to promote agendas of so-called tolerance while ignoring the need for repentance.

As I mentioned in the introduction, in my early days during a James Robison conference, the Spirit poured out on me. I received the anointing to preach to the nations and proclaim the return of Jesus Christ. God told me that He would use me to bring revival to Methodists.

I was so moved that I shared my experience with my District Superintendent. He listened kindly but was not convinced. He responded that Jesus was not really coming back; it was a myth. I was more than surprised by his words. He didn't even believe the Bible was the inspired word of God or that Jesus rose from the dead. I was shocked by his false beliefs, especially because he was a leader of over forty churches in Central Florida.

I thank God that I did not allow the superintendent's unbelief to turn me away from God's calling. Instead, by God's grace, I continued to step out in obedience whenever I heard the Spirit speak to me.

As Peter warned in Second Peter, false teachers and prophets have always existed in the Body of Christ. Jesus also warned that in the last days, the church and the world would be filled with false Christs, prophets, and teachers.

My life has been glorious as God performed so many miracles that this book could not contain them all. I've also witnessed demonic attacks within the church and from without. Persecution and betrayal humbled me to learn to trust in Jesus Christ alone as the *Lord of Hosts*, the One who fights my battles and commands all of heaven on my behalf.

As Jesus predicted, we live in a time of lawlessness, where the laws of God are replaced with the lies of humans. Yet, just as in Ezekiel 37, where God breathed life into the valley of dry bones, He is now raising up a spiritual army. This revival began with the rebirth of Israel and is spreading as His end-time saints rise across the nations, empowered by the Holy Spirit to proclaim His truth. The message is clear: repent and return to Jesus to love and obey Him. Trust in Jesus alone and receive the gift of eternal life, or remain in your sins and be eternally separated from God.

The second part of the message given to Isaiah in 6:11-13 is not quoted in John 12. That part is for the Jews in

Jerusalem who will experience the terrible desolation by the Babylonian army when it destroys the city and the temple. When I read the words, I see the prophesied destruction of Jerusalem given by Jesus during the week of his betrayal, death, and resurrection. Just as Babylon conquered Jerusalem, so will Rome destroy Jerusalem in 70 AD.

The last part of verse 13 signals hope for the hopelessly defeated people of God. A remnant will remain. Out of this small number will be the Holy Seed, Jesus, born the Savior of His people and the nations of the earth. Then, in Isaiah Chapter 7, Isaiah begins to *go* as God sends him with His message. God's faithful servants are always ready to go wherever and to whomever the Spirit directs.

Desolation Defeated

This message given to Isaiah is a hard word to receive, for it foretells the desolation Jerusalem will experience at the hands of the Babylonians, ending in the destruction of the temple and city. The people of God will go into a 70-year captivity as the Jews are taken away from Jerusalem to Babylon. Only a small number will remain around Jerusalem.

It says that because the people of Jerusalem have hardened their hearts, their condition will worsen: "Until the cities are laid waste and without inhabitants, the houses are without a man, the land is utterly desolate…" (Isaiah 6:11).

Desolation is another important word in understanding Scripture. I see the wilderness along the Jordan River, where the land is barren. I see images of bombed-out buildings where only a shell is left standing. Not all have perished, but little remains.

The imagery of desolation aligns with the prophetic warnings found in Scripture. The prophet Daniel uses the word to describe events surrounding both the first and second coming of Jesus (Daniel 9:24–27). For the first coming, Daniel points to the Messiah's arrival and the events leading to His rejection and crucifixion, marking the spiritual desolation of the people. His prophecy also foretells a time of judgment and desolation connected to Christ's return, when Jesus will restore what has been broken and reign in righteousness. Daniel's vision spans both eras, revealing how desolation is intertwined into the story of the rejection of Christ in His first coming and the promise of ultimate restoration at His return.

One message in Daniel is the same as in Isaiah: Repent and believe in the God of Jesus Christ. Put your faith in Jesus, the *Lord of Hosts*, who died for you, rose from the dead, sits at the right Hand of God, and is coming soon. His love, holiness, and truth will overcome the darkness of Satan and the world.

Two kingdoms are in conflict. Fierce battles are being fought for the soul of humanity, for individuals, communities, and nations. Darkness and deception are great, but Jesus and His kingdom are greater. Choose Jesus, and you will know eternal life in the love of His Father and Jesus Christ, the *Lord of Hosts*. Let His gift of brokenness lead you to the beauty of His holiness and into the intimacy with God you were created to experience.

Identity Restored

God created us for Himself, to serve others, and to reign over the earth in holiness and righteousness. But our sin nature and the influences of family and friends corrupted us and created strongholds that have gripped our lives. Jesus came to give us victory over every area of our lives, to tear down these strongholds and heal our broken hearts. There are two choices: life or death. You can choose faithful love and obedience to Jesus or serving a false god and self-fulfillment for your own gain and vainglory. Turn from sin to a new vision for living for Jesus and His Way.

Recently, I was led by the Spirit to pray a powerful prayer:

> God, restore me to how you created me before
> I was ever conceived in my mother's womb.

I believe so many of our struggles are deep-seated from the time we first lived in our mother's womb. Words and emotions we experienced but could not process until we grew into an older child, then a teenager, and an adult.

Jeremiah 1:5, like Psalm 139, makes it clear that God created us as souls in His image before we were given a physical body. God says, "I knew you before I formed you in your mother's womb." After conception, our soul is placed in that newly formed baby.

Once we are conceived with Adam's DNA, the corruption of sin begins to affect us. That is why the Spirit led me to pray for God to restore me when He first created me.

I have shared this prayer with others to help them gain victory in their life. Daily, I pray these words not only at the start of my day but throughout it. I expand on it with Spirit-led insight so that angels of praise and worship can fill my household. I pray for warring angels to drive away all familiar spirits–spirits that are an abomination to God–and all demonic temptations. I ask God to cover me, my family, ministry partners, and friends with the blood of Jesus. I want to be continuously filled with the Holy Spirit, to be led, empowered, and to be anointed by the Spirit so I may be restored to the image of God.

A close friend with the gift of prophecy, Kenneth Bennet, told me, "God gave you a prophetic prayer." It's not some magic formula. It's a cry from my heart for God to transform me into who He created me to be before I was conceived. I still have a long way to go in my walk in the Spirit, but this prayer gives me strength and victory over familiar spirits that influenced me before I was ever born.

Just as God sends His angels to fight on our behalf, He also strengthens us in our deepest trials. Even Jesus, in His greatest moment of struggle, was strengthened by an angel in the Garden of Gethsemane. 'Not My will, but Yours be done,' He prayed, surrendering fully to God's plan (Luke 22:42).

In his first vision with God, Jacob saw angels ascending and descending on the ladder that stretched from earth to heaven. Angels were with him in his hour of trouble as he fled from his brother Esau, who wanted to kill him. God will send angels for your benefit when the storms of temptation strike you.

The prayer of restoration I mentioned above is one Jesus will answer for you. It is a passageway to discover God's vision for your life. One encounter with Jesus far surpasses a lifetime of religion.

Moses, Isaiah, and Peter were forever changed by their encounters with the *Lord of Hosts*. Their obedience brought deliverance, truth, and revival. Now it's your turn. He is not distant or finished. He is still speaking, still sending, still fighting for His people. The question is not whether He will show up, but whether we will respond as they did: "Here I am." Go in the power of the Holy Spirit. Be His light in the world, defeating the armies that hold generations in bondage, so they may be set free to love Jesus and worship the one true God. The *Lord of Hosts* has called you. Now *go*.

GOING DEEPER | Chapter 4

Reflect & Respond

1. Why do you think Moses reacted reluctantly when God called him to lead the Israelites out of Egypt? Have you ever felt unqualified for something God has asked of you?

2. What is significant about God revealing His name as I AM WHO I AM?

3. Isaiah and Moses both responded to God with the words, "Here I am." What does this phrase communicate? How do you typically respond when God calls you to something difficult?

4. Both Moses and Isaiah had to be purified before they could fulfill their mission—Moses by removing his sandals and Isaiah by burning coal. What does this teach us about holiness and preparation for God's work?

For Further Study & Reflection

1. Moses, Isaiah, and Peter were all transformed by their encounters with the Lord of Hosts. Each went on to fulfill God's purposes. How does knowledge of the Lord of Hosts change how you view your purpose?

2. Read Luke 5:8 and Isaiah 6:5. Peter, like Isaiah, experienced a deep conviction of his sin when encountering Jesus. Why do you think awareness of our brokenness is a key step in being used by God?

3. How does Jackie Pullinger's story illustrate the importance of stepping out in faith, even when the details are unclear?

4. Isaiah's message to the people was often ignored, just as many religious leaders rejected Jesus's words. Why do you think people resist God's truth?

5. Read Isaiah 6:11-13. How does God bring hope and restoration out of desolation?

6. Read Isaiah 6:5-7 and Luke 5:8-10. The parallel between Isaiah's response and Peter's calling reminds us that lives are forever changed when God speaks. However, each had to experience brokenness before stepping into their calling. How does surrendering to God allow Him to bring out the God potential in your life? What might He be calling you to surrender today

7. Read John 1:42 and Luke 5:10-11. When Jesus called Peter, Jesus saw his God potential—who he would become through faith and obedience. How does recognizing your God potential change how you see yourself and your purpose?

While Moses, Isaiah, and Peter were changed by divine encounters, their transformation pointed to something even greater. Each moment of surrender prepared the way for the fulfillment of a promise– a promise sealed not by fire or vision, but by blood. The call to *go* begins with an encounter, but it is the cross that completes the mission.

5

The Promise

Each time the crown of thorns was pressed against His brow, Jesus saw the salvation of the human race. It was a vision that coursed through the depths of His being. The intense pain from the whip, embedded with bone and sharp metal, tore at His flesh, pushing Jesus to His limit. With each lash across His back, He derived hope from Isaiah's words, "By His stripes, we are healed." (Isaiah 53:5).

Hanging on the cross for the sins of the world reminded Jesus of God's promise to humanity to send a Savior to crush the head of the serpent, Satan. Humanity's only hope of redemption rested upon Him, the Lord of Hosts, who shed His blood to fulfill the covenant and triumph over the powers of darkness.

The agony tempted Jesus to cry out for His army of angels to wipe out the Roman legions, but He resisted because of His greater love. Even in His suffering, Jesus remained the Lord of Hosts, restraining His power out of love, not weakness.

God had promised Abraham that his Seed would bring salvation to his descendants and the world. All this enabled Jesus to endure with joy even as His blood flowed.

Despite the ongoing rebellion and idolatry of God's people, the Creator remained faithful to His Word. His only begotten Son fulfilled hundreds of prophecies. Yet, even greater suffering was still to come. The oneness Jesus knew with His Father was shattered in a moment of separation. When Jesus took our sins upon Himself, God forsook Him so His blood could wash away our sins.

In the torture of that division, Jesus cried out, "My God, My God, why have You forsaken Me?" (Matthew 27:46, Mark 15:34). Despite the agony of separation as He bore the full weight of sin, Jesus remained faithful to His Father's redemptive plan. He knew His Father in heaven accepted His sacrifice. It was finished. Humanity was saved from itself and bondage to Satan. We now experience the wonder of eternal life because we can know the one true God and the Son He sent. The promise to Abraham was fulfilled.

Jesus then rose from the dead as the one sign that He was the Anointed One, destined to deliver us from our sins. Through Him, we are reconciled with God.

Nothing is impossible with God.

God's Glory Fulfilled

Jesus's suffering was not an isolated event. It was the fulfillment of centuries of prophetic warnings and promises, as seen throughout the book of Isaiah. In

Chapters 7 and 8, nations are under God's judgment, but the Lord of Hosts protects His people, even when they have lost their way. Our Creator's goal of redemption never changes. When Adam sinned, God promised to redeem him and Eve; it was individual salvation. When Noah's generation fell into idolatry and evil, He promised to redeem families. When He called Abraham, the father of many nations, He promised to redeem nations and individuals through his seed, Jesus Christ. It is a repeated reminder of salvation in the Bible.

All through Isaiah, God promises to redeem and restore Israel. The *Lord of Hosts* turns His fury upon those who have afflicted Israel. In Chapter 44, the *Lord of Hosts* is described as the Lord, the King of Israel, the Redeemer of Israel, the First and the Last. He plans to blot out Jacob's sins, redeem Israel, and restore Jerusalem, Judah, and the temple. Jesus is faithful to fulfill His promises. It's a truth found throughout all of Scripture.

Jesus saves those who answer His call. However, He also promises to judge those who reject Him. Eternal life or eternal separation from God are the only two destinies. There will be no place for bargaining or excuses. Jesus makes that absolutely clear.

Isaiah Chapter 7 sets the stage for redemption with the promise of a virgin who will conceive and have a child, Immanuel–God with us. Then, Chapter 9 builds upon the prophecy by revealing the true nature and mission of this Child. It offers a fuller revelation of God's redemptive plan through the promised Child, who is like no other baby.

> "For unto us a Child is born,
> Unto us a Son is given;
> And the government will be upon His shoulder.
> And His name will be called
> Wonderful, Counselor, Mighty God,
> Everlasting Father, Prince of Peace." (Isaiah 9:6)

No mere human can qualify for this description. This Child will grow up to be the Lamb of God and the Lion of Judah, God's anointed One. Only God incarnate can fulfill this role. He is the ultimate King and Savior whose role is to bring redemption to the world. He is the forever Ruler who brings everlasting peace, justice, and righteousness to all who have yielded to Him.

When reading Isaiah 9:6, I want to fall on my face before Jesus to worship and love Him. I want to thank Him for who He is and all He has done for me and all of humanity. As Revelation 5:12-13 confirms, Jesus alone is worthy of our worship and adoration as He sits at the right hand of the Father.

Later in Isaiah, Jesus will be exalted as God's suffering Servant. John 12:37-38 quotes Isaiah 53:1, "Who has believed our report? And to whom has the arm of the Lord been revealed?" This verse emphasizes the rejection Jesus faced despite all the evidence that He was who He professed to be. Isaiah 53:3 goes on to describe Jesus in detail as the One who came from heaven to earth to endure the torment of being "despised and rejected by men, a Man of sorrows and acquainted with grief."

This King, whose crown was made of thorns, endured being tortured by men so that He could die for our sins.

Let me remind you, Jesus could have called for the legions of angels who are at His command to save Him. Yet, out of love for us, He laid down His life so that the love of God could redeem us.

The titles and names given to Jesus throughout the Bible tell us of the nature and character of this God who alone is God. There are no other gods, just false idols and demons seeking to seduce us from our eternal destiny.

Jesus, in Isaiah 9:6-7, promises to remove all evil and wickedness and restore God's glory over all of the earth. The peace of God will reign from the throne of Jesus in the hearts of every human over all of creation. It's what we long for but can never achieve by our own efforts.

God's People Preserved

Israel and the Jewish people are the conduits of bringing forth this promise God first made to Adam, then to Noah, and finally to Abraham. Throughout history, all the efforts of Satan and humanity have never been able to stop God's vision from unfolding.

No wonder we live in a time when many nations and peoples are trying to destroy the Jews and permanently remove Israel as a nation. Almost every country in the Middle East and Europe has persecuted the Jews under the illusion of Satan's deception. Even Christians and Muslims have fallen for the Devil's lies to kill and torture the Jewish people.

God's promises to preserve Israel have been challenged throughout history. Nevertheless, no ancient or modern force has succeeded in erasing His people. The atrocities of World War II serve as a stark reminder of this ongoing battle, fulfilling the prophetic warnings of Scripture.

This evil reached its height under Adolf Hitler's Nazi regime. During World War II, Hitler wanted to establish alliances with certain Arab leaders who shared anti-Zionist sentiments. A prominent figure in this collaboration was an Islamic religious leader, Amin al-Husseini, the Grand Mufti of Jerusalem. In a meeting on November 28, 1941, al-Husseini and Hitler discussed their mutual opposition to the establishment of a Jewish homeland in Palestine. Al-Husseini sought assurances from Germany's leader to support the prevention of such a homeland, to which Hitler responded that his country's objective was the genocide of all of the Jews, including those living in Arab lands under the protection of the British. [1] [2]

Furthermore, Nazi propaganda efforts extended to the Middle East, aiming to incite anti-Jewish sentiment and gain support among Arab populations. Arabic-language broadcasts and literature were disseminated to emphasize common enemies: Zionists, those in support of a Jewish homeland, and the British. The propaganda often included translations of Hitler's *Mein Kampf*, which made clear his vision for the elimination of Jews. [3]

Today, this plan of destruction continues as Iran and its terrorist proxies, Hamas and Hezbollah, pursue their onslaught against Israel. Even the turning of the United Nations against the tiny country fulfills the biblical prophecy that all the nations of the earth will come against Israel (Zechariah 12:3).

Isaiah prophesied about these events over 2,700 years ago, foretelling the fate of nations surrounding Israel. God's promise of deliverance has remained steadfast, miraculously resisting this relentless tide of war. Even the brutal attack on October 7, 2023, when Hamas carried out the surprise massacre of innocent Jews, served as a grim reminder of Isaiah's warnings. In Isaiah 34, God pronounces judgment on the nations responsible for crimes against Israel.

In Isaiah's day, God miraculously saved the Jewish people. Over the next 700 years, before Jesus was born—and continuing to the present and into the future before His return, the Jews have been and will be preserved. In Isaiah 48:11, God says, "And I will not give My glory to another." His plan of salvation will never fail. Despite the sins and treachery of Israel's people, God will save them for His name's sake. Thus, despite facing overwhelming enemies, persecution, and wars, Israel has survived. It will never be wiped from the face of the earth.

Nevertheless, the evil will not stop against the Jews and Israel until Jesus returns. Up until the end of this age, Jerusalem will be surrounded by enemies. Then Jesus, the *Lord of Hosts*, will come and destroy all who have persecuted His people.

When we understand Israel's prophetic role, our faith in God's sovereignty deepens. Just as He has preserved Israel against all odds, He remains faithful to His promises to us today.

God's Promises Endure

Isaiah 9:6 gives us a vivid description of a Savior who will perform all the wonders that will establish His reign forever. As the *Lord of Hosts*, He will bring justice and peace to the world.

In the prophetic context, the Babylonian Empire, the "bird of prey from the east," is called by God to carry out His will swiftly. (Isaiah 46:11) He is giving His people another opportunity to repent. Babylon serves as both a tool of divine judgment and a symbol of exile and suffering for Israel. However, Babylon will be humbled and destroyed because its rulers showed God's people no mercy.

Today's Babylon–not a single geographic location but a global system driven by greed, immorality, and rebellion against God–will also fall. It is a prophecy that is reiterated in Revelation, not just for one city and one nation, but for the entire world system of Babylon, Satan's kingdom that sought to dominate Israel and the world.

Yet, in the end, Israel will be refined as "fine silver" (Isaiah 48:10). The refiner is the *Lord of Hosts*, Jesus, the Messiah. He will fulfill God's ancient prophecies of redemption for His people and the Gentiles from every nation. The Holy One of Israel led His heavenly armies to destroy ancient Babylon and will lead them again to destroy the terrorists and nations surrounding Israel. In the latter days, as recorded in Revelation 19, He will bring final judgment upon all the kings and armies that rebel against God.

Israel, reborn as a nation in 1948, makes clear the promise of the Savior. Never again shall the Jews lose their nation. With unwavering resolve, they will fight for Israel's survival—the living God and His Word guarantee this endurance.

Even today, the Creator continues to refine Israel from its sins. Israel seems much like America in its spirituality and secular humanism. While there is great faith, there are also many false gods and philosophies permeating each land. In the last days, as Isaiah, Paul, and Jesus prophesied, the Jewish people will know their Deliverer, the *Lord of Hosts*, Jesus Christ. He will be victorious and reign in their forever.

God's Justice Reigns

In June 2024, my wife, Beverly, and I went to the Gaza border to see personally the evil that was perpetrated on Israel on October 7. Our good friend, Jonathan Feldstein, and an elite sniper from the Israel Defense Forces (IDF), led us. We visited several locations where the atrocities took place: the site of the Nova Music Festival, a kibbutz, and a graveyard of vehicles destroyed by Hamas.

As we walked through the kibbutz, a thought plagued me: *Where are the American and European news agencies to tell this horror story?* Instead, the propaganda of the enemy held sway over the truth. The stories we heard of the torture and destruction of families and homes left me angry and sad. Only Satan could instill such evil in the minds of the terrorists.

Words fail to describe the carnage that was unleashed that day. The celebrations by people and nations across the globe were shocking. Even on elite U.S. college campuses like Columbia and Harvard, anti-Israel protests replaced attending classes for some students. That is why filmed details and recorded stories need to be seen. Yet, even after viewing unedited footage, many denied the truth because Satan blinded them.

General Dwight D. Eisenhower, "unprepared for the Nazi brutality he witnessed at Ohrdruf concentration camp in April 1945," warned of a time when there would be those who denied the horrors. So, "he invited the media to document the scene and compelled Germans living in the surrounding towns and any soldier not fighting at the front to witness the atrocities for themselves." [4] In a letter to General George C. Marshall, Eisenhower wrote that he visited the camp to "give first-hand evidence" because "there develops a tendency" to describe atrocities as propaganda. [5]

The future president had the foresight to understand that we must never forget what was done to the Jews by Hitler and his henchmen. We all must confront evil, or it will win many of the battles waged before our Lord returns. We can be assured, however, that the *Lord of Hosts* will banish evil forever from His domain. He is the only one capable of such an achievement. No world leader or nation can do what Jesus will do. He will fulfill God's promise to the men and women of the Bible.

The *Lord of Hosts* will come in His glory, leading the armies of heaven against Satan, his demons, and rebellious kings. In righteousness, He will judge and make war. (Revelation 19:11) He will destroy all evil and unholiness to create a new heaven and earth. The slaughter of all that is evil will be final; there will be no reversal of the ultimate act of judgment. The gates of hell cannot withstand the *Lord of Hosts'* restoration of holiness and the love of God. Then, as Revelation 7 tells us, the Jewish people will lead the worship in heaven as the Gentile believers surround the throne of God in worship. The promise of salvation will be fulfilled.

God's Power Revealed

As I described earlier, rebellion is like radioactive material that must be completely removed to ensure a safe world. The Prince of Peace will remove all rebellion against God.

> "Of the increase of *His* government and peace
>
> *There will be* no end,
>
> Upon the throne of David and over His kingdom,
>
> To order it and establish it with judgment and justice
>
> From that time forward, even forever.
>
> The zeal of the *Lord of Hosts* will perform this." (Isaiah 9:7)

By the blood of Jesus Christ, the promise in God's eternal covenant with Adam, Noah, and Abraham will do what no one else can do. All things will be made new, as Isaiah and John prophesied. Everyone can receive the promise. All can know the love of God that sustains us and carries us from death to life. Jesus is the Resurrection and the Life.

One of the most important promises of the blood covenant, the New Covenant of Jesus Christ, is the gift of the Holy Spirit and fire. John the Baptist, in John Chapter 1, tells us Jesus is the Lamb of God who came to take away the sin of the world. He came to give us the gift of the Holy Spirit and fire to transform, empower, and teach us how to follow Jesus.

Isaiah 11:2 prophesied how the Spirit will rest on Jesus and that this Spirit is one of understanding, might, and knowledge. In the Book of Luke, we are told of four major works of the Holy Spirit that enabled Jesus to do His ministry among His people.

- He was filled with the Spirit (Luke 4:1).
- He was led by the Spirit (Luke 4:1).
- He was empowered by the Spirit (Luke 4:14).
- He was anointed by the Spirit to fulfill the purposes of God (Luke 4:18).

Too many followers of Jesus have forgotten this promise of the Holy Spirit. He has become an intellectual truth instead of an active presence in their lives. Only by the power of the Holy Spirit can we live out God's promises to prepare the way for Jesus's return.

Jesus told His disciples to ask for the Holy Spirit and to wait for Him to be poured into their lives. On the Day of Pentecost, the Spirit came like a mighty wind from heaven. Throughout the Book of Acts, Jesus's followers experience the baptism of the Holy Spirit and the call to be His witnesses in Jerusalem, Judea, Samaria, and to the ends of the earth.

What began in Jerusalem will end in Jerusalem when Jesus returns, as prophesied by Isaiah. He tells how the Messiah will pour the Holy Spirit on Himself. Then, in the last days, the Spirit will be poured upon the Jewish people, and all Israel will be saved.

The history of Israel testifies to the faithfulness of God. Throughout the generations, God has promised to restore and redeem Israel against impossible odds. No human could do what God has done for Israel and those who follow Jesus Christ. What God promises will come to pass. No one can hinder His will.

Jesus and His Father continue to pour out the Holy Spirit daily all over the earth. I have seen entire churches of people baptized in the Spirit in Cuba, Pakistan, and Zambia. One of the most recent was in Las Tunas, Cuba. Our team attended different churches each night, where everyone lifted their hands to heaven to be baptized with the Holy Spirit. Another time I saw His power firsthand was during a mission trip to Zambia.

God's Glory Experienced

Zambia's rainy season translates to downpours, making it nearly impossible for people to walk to church. The unpaved roads are mud pits; the pathways become pools. The rain pounding on the tin roofs drowns out the message. Yet, one year, just as God called Jackie Pullinger to *go*, He called me to *go* during this torrential time of year.

Each night, as we gathered for worship, my longtime friend and missionary, Delbert, and I prayed in faith that the rain would hold back so the people could attend church. And for two weeks, God answered. Though the skies threatened, the rain never fell near us during the services.

On the final night, we met at the John Wesley Chapel. I was led to lift up the promises of God. I reminded the people about how God answered Moses's cry for His glory, He fulfilled His covenant through Jesus, and He continues to reveal His power to those who seek Him.

When we got to the close of the message, I was about to give an altar call for those who wanted to give their life to Jesus, when suddenly the glory of God–the weight of His majesty and wonder–descended upon us. Overcome by His holiness, we found ourselves lying prostrate on the dirt floor. Then, the sound of weeping and wailing filled the air. God's glory convicted us of our sins. For over half an hour, we lay in His presence, the Spirit cleansing and renewing every heart. When we rose, puddles of tears dampened the dirt floor. God met us there. When we stepped outside, raindrops finally began to fall.

Later, as Delbert and I reflected on what we had witnessed, he shared how the Zambian Methodist churches had grown from just a handful to over 250 in the past 20 years. When people in the U.S. ask him why American churches are shrinking while Zambia's are increasing, his answer is simple: "The tears of glory."

No matter how often I hear people cry out and see them encounter the glory of God, I'm always profoundly touched by the incredible experience. If we truly desire to see God's promises fulfilled in our lives, we must seek Him with everything in us. The tears of glory that fell that night in Zambia were a testimony—a reminder that when we surrender to Him, He reveals His power, presence, and faithfulness, just as He always has.

Let the fullness of the promise be real in your life. Ask and believe, and then receive all that God has promised you. Your life will be changed, and you will see the glory of God.

Come, Lord Jesus, come. Fulfill Your promise to Adam, Noah, and Abraham by coming in Your glory to make all things new. Pour out the Holy Spirit upon us. Bring us to the brokenness of surrender and trust in Jesus. The *Lord of Hosts* will end the curse and invite us to live in the blessings of God's promise of eternal life with Him.

GOING DEEPER | Chapter 5

Reflect & Respond

1. Read Isaiah 7:14. How does the fulfillment of this prophecy demonstrate God's faithfulness to His people throughout history?

2. Read Isaiah 9:6-7. What do the titles given to Jesus reveal about His authority and purpose? How do they affirm His role as the ultimate King?

3. Read Isaiah 53:5. How does the description of what Christ would suffer demonstrate His power and love? How does this change the way you view difficulties in your own life?

4. Jesus could have called upon legions of angels to rescue Him from the cross, but chose to fulfill the Father's plan. How does His restraint as the commander of heavenly armies reveal the depth of His love for humanity?

For Further Study & Reflection

1. Read Isaiah 48:11. How does the Lord of Hosts' protection of Israel reflect His ongoing faithfulness to His covenant?

2. Read John 12:37-38. How does this passage highlight the rejection Jesus faced? Why do people struggle to believe even when faced with the truth?

3. Read Revelation 5:12-13. How does the heavenly worship of Jesus reflect the fulfillment of God's promise through Him?

4. Read Revelation 19:11. How does this verse reference Jesus, the Lord of Hosts? How does knowing that He will ultimately triumph over evil shape your perspective on current world events and personal struggles?

5. Read Isaiah 46:11. How does the assurance that the Lord of Hosts is sovereign throughout history give you confidence in His promises for your life? How can you live in alignment with His eternal plan?

God's call is never about the one being called—it's about His greater plan. Moses was chosen to lead the Israelites out of slavery, and Isaiah was sent to call a nation back to holiness. But their missions were only glimpses of what was to come: Jesus, the *Lord of Hosts*, bearing the weight of sin for all people.

6

The Return

The dark stable reeked of animal dung and old hay. Soon, it would be filled with cries of birth pangs announcing the arrival of a newborn son. The young mother pushed aside her fears about her first child being born with only the help of her husband.

Between each painful contraction, she recalled her encounter nine months earlier when an angel told her she would conceive a child by the Holy Spirit. Even more amazing was that this child would be the world's Savior. The angel announced that the Creator had chosen her to give birth to Immanuel, God with us, and to name Him Jesus, for He will save His people from their sins.

Her fear vanished in the beauty and comfort of the angel's words of hope and life. Although she had many questions and few answers, Mary trusted in God for her protection.

When the same angel appeared in her fiancé Joseph's dream, he, too, was assured that the child was from God. Together, they faced the gossip concerning the unwed pregnancy, which could have led to her being stoned to death. Their encounters with God through the angel gave them the faith to rejoice in this precious gift of life.

With one last push, the pain turned to joy when she held her child in her arms. She pondered how this innocent baby could be the hope of humanity. Then, the night sky was filled with light from the Lord, and a chorus of angels shone brightly, announcing to the world that the King of Heaven had been born.

"Glory to God in the highest, and on earth peace, goodwill to men" (Luke 2:14). The King had come as an infant who grew into a man who was rejected by Israel's Jewish leaders and the Roman governor, Pontius Pilate. Heaven's beings marveled at the folly of men.

His Return

Jesus's birth was only His first arrival. Remember, Isaiah received his calling to be God's visionary in Isaiah Chapter 6. Judah's king had died, but the prophet saw the eternal King of Israel on the throne in the temple, the *Lord of Hosts*. Isaiah's vision pointed to the promise of a King from David's line who would bring hope to God's people. Centuries later, the promise was fulfilled when Jesus was born in humble circumstances.

Jesus, the King of Kings and Commander of Heaven's Armies, will come once again. Yet, multitudes mock the prophecy that He will leave His heavenly throne to return again to Earth. When He returns, He will come in such glory and power that, in the end, every knee will bow, and every tongue will confess that Jesus is Lord.

According to Jesus's own prophetic words, most will be unprepared because they have neglected God's purposes. They will discover that the Holy One will usher in His kingdom for all who have loved and obeyed Him. The faithful will receive His free gift of eternal life.

The reality of His coming will shake the world, and many will deeply regret it. However, those He knows will rejoice in the Light of His glory. They answered the question of faith Jesus asked, "*Who do you say that I am?*" Peter answered in Matthew 16:15-16, "*You are the Christ, the Son of the living God.*" Those who answer as Peter did will enter into God's eternal kingdom—a place void of sin and death and full of love and life.

From the beginning, God's Word has revealed who Jesus is. Isaiah, centuries before Christ's birth, recorded names that declare His identity for all eternity:

- Lord of Hosts
- Mighty God
- Prince of Peace
- The Root of Jesse
- The Son of David
- Everlasting Father

Isaiah's faith was in the *Lord of Hosts*, the *King of kings* and *Lord of lords*, the One whose kingdom will never end.

One night, while in prayer, I was led to write the following statements. They remind me that Jesus Christ is God as prophesied throughout the Bible, and we can trust Him alone for our salvation, regardless of world events.

- He is the Son of God.
- He is the *Lord of Hosts.*
- He is risen from the dead.
- He is alive forevermore.
- He sits at the right Hand of God.
- He is coming again.

His Justice

There is no doubt that Jesus is the Savior of the world. The reality of who Jesus Christ is can only be grasped by faith. There is no proof against Him. The evidence confirms that He is God who became man. However, until you have experienced the Prince of Peace, you can't know Him. And to know Him is eternal life. The truth can be mocked, and the reality denied, but it does not change who He is.

Jesus is the great *I Am* that Moses met in the burning bush. Jesus is the *Lord of Hosts* whom Isaiah encountered in the temple. Jesus is the risen One the apostles met three days after He was crucified. Jesus is the Master of human history, as John wrote in Revelation. Jesus is the God of glory who transformed Saul into the great Apostle Paul. Jesus is the greatest visionary. He made fishermen and tax collectors into spiritual giants who were empowered to change the world through our glorious Redeemer.

One day soon, Jesus will come in His glory to remove all sin, evil, and death from the human race. He will make all things new: a new heaven and a new earth. Everyone who believes will dwell in the light and glory of His Presence forever.

Many scoff at what I just wrote, but the truth is, Jesus is the Son of God. He is God, and He is the only way to salvation. Our Lord is the fulfillment of God's covenant promise to King David that His descendant will sit on the throne of Israel forever. Jesus, as Isaiah prophesied in Chapter 11, comes from the Branch of Jesse. This promised ruler will reign forever, not only over Israel but over all the nations, bringing peace to the entire earth.

Isaiah describes this ruler as one filled with "the Spirit of wisdom and understanding," who judges "with righteousness" and brings justice "for the meek of the earth." He strikes the wicked "with the rod of His mouth," and wears righteousness and faithfulness like a belt (Isaiah 11:2–5).

This is no passive figure. Isaiah's vision points to the Commander of Heaven's Armies who will return to wage war against all evil and establish His kingdom of truth and peace.

You may ask, "What about those who never heard of Him?" That's not your concern. A merciful God will take care of that situation. Your concern should be your answer, for you have heard of Him. You have eternal life if He knows you and you know Him as Lord and Savior.

If you don't know Jesus, then He does not know you. Your destiny is eternal separation from God. You may think, "That's not fair. It's not right." Yet, Jesus clarifies there will be no debate over who He is on judgment day or what you argue in your defense. Isaiah foretold it, and John saw it in Revelation. On the Day of the Lord, those who have rejected Jesus will cry out for the rocks to fall upon them in fear of His judgment (Isaiah 2:19, Revelation 6:15-17).

This fear comes when they finally acknowledge Jesus as the King of kings, who holds absolute authority and power. Unlike worldly leaders, He does not abuse or misuse power. Instead, Jesus acts guided by holiness and righteousness. He is the One True Judge, dispensing perfect justice in ways beyond our comprehension.

The themes of judgment and mercy are woven throughout Scripture. In Isaiah 10, we see God bringing judgment on His people, the Jews, for their rebellion. Yet, even in judgment, God demonstrates His mercy. He spares a remnant through whom He will fulfill the promise of salvation, not just for the Jews but also for the Gentiles.

This connection between the judgment of the present and the hope of the future is central to God's plan. While His holiness requires justice, His love ensures that His covenant promises are fulfilled. In Jesus, judgment and mercy meet, offering salvation to all who trust Him.

His Righteousness

When studying the history of Israel and its kings, it would seem impossible for one of David's descendants to become king. Why? The conquests of Israel by the Babylonians, the Greeks, and the Romans destroyed David's royal lineage. Thus, none of his descendants continued sitting on the throne. His ruling line all but disappeared.

Yet, the Jews have a tradition of meticulously maintaining genealogical records, enabling the apostle Matthew to trace Jesus's genealogy to David. When the Jews hailed Jesus as the Son of David upon entering Jerusalem, it clearly indicated His Messianic identity.

Isaiah points to a righteous ruler who will defeat wickedness, though he saw only a glimpse of Jesus's glory. One day, the Lion of Judah will return and reign from Jerusalem as our eternal King, revealing the fullness of His power. In Revelation 19, John describes this *Lord of Hosts* as the One who comes to rid the world of all evil and unholiness. What a glorious day it will be when He defeats every enemy of God and establishes His everlasting reign. Those who denied and rejected Him will be silenced forever in the eternal fires of hell.

In Luke 3, we learn that the Holy Spirit descends upon Jesus after He is water-baptized. It symbolized that Jesus, though sinless, was to fulfill all righteousness and identify with humanity in its need for repentance. In the next chapter of Luke, we learn that Jesus, empowered by the Holy Spirit, begins His ministry as promised by Isaiah.

Throughout His life before the cross and resurrection, He offered people a new vision for living—one grounded in faith in His identity and mission. To the adulterous woman, Jesus said, "Go and sin no more." Zacchaeus, the hated tax collector, discovered he could be accepted, and because He believed in Jesus, he paid restitution to those he had cheated. To fishermen like Simon, Jesus brought out their *God potential* to change the world. The leper healed and cleansed would no longer be an outcast in society but a witness to who Jesus was.

This new life took root in their love for Jesus, nurtured by the brokenness that opened the way to greater intimacy with God. That kind of transformation doesn't end with the Scriptures. One such story is about a man named Adrian, whose life impacted many.

His Vision

Adrian stood alone on the football field. He cried into the night in response to Jesus's call for him to become a pastor. He wanted to be empowered by the Holy Spirit to lead people to faith in Jesus.

But the Spirit told him, "You are not low enough to receive such power. "

Adrian fell to his knees and cried out to God again. Once more, the Spirit told him he was not low enough. From his knees, he fell on his face in the grass and asked God for the fullness of the Spirit.

"You are not low enough," the Spirit spoke. With his hands, he pulled up the grass and dirt to lie face down in a hole and said, "I can't get any lower." Then, the Spirit was poured out upon the young man, who became one of the great preachers of the twentieth century.

Like He did with Adrian Rogers, God calls each of us to the same level of brokenness. Once we get there, we can be the best Spirit-filled parent, businessperson, teacher, truck driver, judge, or whatever God has led us to be. We can do our part to change the world for Jesus.

When traveling the world, I share with people a new vision for living rooted in faith in Jesus as their Savior. Everywhere, people are in bondage to human traditions. Generations of indoctrination in false gods and religion have trapped them in a culture of oppression and hopelessness.

Just as Jesus gave the blind a new vision for living, He does that today for the world's poor. He takes away their fears as He washes away their sins. In Him, they find hope and a new life full of purpose.

Jesus completed all anyone needs for their new life by dying on the cross in their place. His call is for each of us to turn from our old ways to His new ways of living. He offers a life full of love, joy, and peace. Because we are filled with His Holy Spirit, we can withstand the storms of life.

The first time I shared the truth of Jesus was with a single woman who visited the church I was attending. Three of us went to her apartment to welcome her and to talk about Jesus. My heart was pounding as I shared about Jesus and eternal life. I was fearful she would reject what I said about our need for God's forgiveness. Yet, after I told her about Jesus's love for her and her need to repent of her sins, she fell on her knees and said, " I have been looking for Jesus all of my life."

To be honest, I was stunned. I was so new at sharing Jesus with another person that I didn't expect such a demonstration of surrender and faith.

Since that night, I have been blessed to share the Good News of Jesus Christ—the *Lord of Hosts* —with millions through television, podcasts, articles, books, social media, crusades, and personal conversations. I have also had the privilege of seeing how Jesus transforms lives.

His Gift

One of my favorite memories was visiting Chief Kanyama of the Lunda tribe in Zambia. He is one of seven chiefs ruling these beautiful people.

Our drive to the Lunda tribal lands was long and difficult. The two-lane road was riddled with potholes due to inadequate infrastructure and the massive weight of the trucks carrying copper from the mines. In some places, springs bubbled up through the pavement. Dodging back and forth to avoid breaking an axle felt like navigating Pac-Man's maze.

When we finally reached the town of Mwinilunga, we turned onto a dirt road surrounded by lush vegetation. This road had been graded in most places, but it was slow going, especially when we came to the bridges crossing the rivers. One was so rickety that the other passengers and I refused to stay in the vehicle, so we walked across. The van followed behind us. Below, in the swirling river waters, lay a truck that had flipped off the bridge. The hippos and crocodiles who claimed the river as their own were oblivious to it.

Finally, we reached the village to meet the chief and his wonderful people. Upon entering his palace, we bowed before him. Even though bodyguards surrounded him, we received a warm welcome. Through a translator, we talked of his kingdom and his faith in Jesus Christ.

About an hour into our conversation, we were interrupted. One of the chief's men entered the room and whispered in his ear. He then informed us there was a villager they feared had just died. Although I didn't fully grasp the situation, I agreed to accompany them to the villager's home. While on the way, the chief's prime minister shared that the "dead" man was the chief's "worthless alcoholic" son, Gibbs. If Gibbs was still alive, the prime minister hoped my prayer would change his life.

Villagers packed the house, making it hard to breathe. My brother in Christ and fellow missionary, Delbert, and I were the only white people. Gibbs lay passed out on the floor with drool pooling around his mouth. It was hard to think of it as pathetic since he was thankfully alive. I couldn't imagine losing a child.

The tension in the room made it feel even more stifling. I felt as if everyone was staring at me, challenging me. *What can this white man do? Is he truly a man of God?*

I prayed silently. The Spirit answered. I was to cast out demons.

I raised my voice—not in fear, but in authority through Jesus—and commanded the demons to leave. The room fell quiet, heavy with the presence of God.

As the demons departed, Gibbs awakened. He was startled when he looked up to see a stranger's face, a white one at that. Once revived, he became aware of all the people who had congregated in his home.

As I talked to him, he seemed to be sober, which was fortunate because we had something important to talk about—Jesus. Gibbs told me he wanted to be delivered from his addiction and become a follower of Jesus. Right there, he prayed to ask forgiveness and gave his heart to Jesus. I commanded the spirit of alcoholism to leave him.

His wife and mother were both in the room, so I told him he needed to ask for their forgiveness. He did. I'll never forget the intensity and glory of this moment. It seemed everyone was in tears. The villagers marveled at what God had done for this troubled man and his sinful ways.

We never know the outcome after such an encounter with the *Lord of Hosts,* whose power commands the forces of heaven. Yet, at every service, Gibbs showed up sober. When we returned the next year, he was not only sober but was singing in the choir and working at the village school. When we visited the third year, he attended all the revival meetings and became a leader at the school. His marriage was strong, and his children were blessed.

Jesus Christ transformed this man. The gift of eternal life was real for him. I ask you again, "Who do you say Jesus is?" Every year, millions of people across the globe answer, as Gibbs answered, "He is the Son of God, my Lord and Savior, whom I love and follow."

His Light

The same *Lord of Hosts* who transformed Gibbs's life was first revealed to Isaiah in a vision—a King who would one day rule in justice and righteousness. That King was born in a dark, quiet stable and spent His life offering new vision and hope to the broken. From Zacchaeus to the leper, He transformed lives and brought the light of God's kingdom to earth.

Jesus said He is the Light of the world. He dispels the darkness of evil so the truth of God can reign in our lives. We try hard not to admit that we are full of deceit and darkness. To paraphrase Luke 7:21, out of our hearts flows a multitude of sins.

Nevertheless, the battle between good and evil did not end with Jesus's resurrection. Though His victory is assured, we continue to see the devastating reach of sin in our world. From violent conflicts to the destruction of innocent lives, the same forces that rejected Christ now seek to destroy His truth and people. This reality is painfully clear in the suffering of those caught in war and terrorism, especially in Israel, where the consequences of hatred and deception are undeniable.

Because of my ministry work in Israel, I receive constant updates on what is happening there. Each time Hamas releases the bodies of hostages, I feel the sorrow of the Israelis. It is as though the weight of death has fallen upon the nation. It feels like we are reliving the slaughter of the innocents recorded in Jeremiah 31:15 and Matthew 2:16-18.

That phrase—*the slaughter of the innocents*—was first used to describe the horrific actions of King Herod, and after hearing from the wise men that a new king had been born in Bethlehem, Herod, threatened by the prophecy, ordered that every male child from newborn to two be put to death. His order fulfilled the words of Jeremiah: "A voice was heard in Ramah, Lamentation, weeping, and great mourning, Rachel weeping for her children, refusing to be comforted because they are no more" (Matthew 2:18).

One especially painful story among many resulting from the October 7 attack on Israel by Hamas is that of Shiri Bibas. The terrified mother was "seen swaddling her two redheaded boys in a blanket and being whisked away by armed men." The video of their being taken hostage "ricocheted around the world in the hours after the attack." Almost two years later, the bodies of Ariel, who had been four when he was kidnapped, and Kfir, less than a year old, were finally returned. Hamas claimed the children died during an Israeli air attack. The autopsy showed they were strangled. What of their mother? As of this writing, we don't know. The body in her casket was that of an unknown Palestinian woman. [1]

In 2008, while in Israel with a team of 30 from our church, I heard a Holocaust survivor share her experience. She was one of the approximately 1200 names on Oskar Schindler's list. One graphic recollection she shared was when Nazis stormed her apartment building and threw Jewish babies out the windows.

What kind of monsters could throw babies to their deaths? Strangle babies in the name of God? Evil does exist, and through the centuries, history has proven humanity is capable of great wickedness. Numerous studies have been conducted on how ordinary individuals can be convinced to carry out atrocities. Yet, people just like you and me performed such heinous acts.

It's difficult to write about these atrocities. Yet, much of the world is applauding the evil of Hamas. Many either rationalize the brutality of their actions or deny them. There is no defense for the terror they have inflicted.

Hamas has taught the children for nearly twenty years in Gaza that Jews are sub-human and must be killed no matter the cost. Children have been taught in schools, often supported by U.S. grant money, to hate and murder the Jews. Songs are sung about death to the Israelis.

This barbarism can only be ended by defeating Hamas and all terrorists. Their brainwashing efforts must be reversed through reeducation and, even more effectively, by the love of Jesus Christ. One story I received is a testament to this. A woman who was raised to hate the Jews and who believed the Holocaust never happened met Jesus. The Light of Jesus removed the darkness from her soul, and she discovered the truth about Israel. Now, as a former Muslim, she is teaching others about the terrorists and their lies.

Though evil persists, Jesus actively pushes back the darkness, rescuing, redeeming, and leading His people with power and purpose. So, how do you combat evil? With Jesus Christ, the *Lord of Hosts*.

The Lion of Judah will return to defeat evil once and for all, ushering in a new heaven and earth. His eternal reign will be a time of joy, peace, and perfect justice. So, I ask you, "Who do you say Jesus is? Have you bowed before Him to surrender your heart and to trust in Him alone for your salvation? If you have, then pray to be His Light in this world of evil. His love and truth will prevail.

GOING DEEPER | Chapter 6

Reflect & Respond

1. Jesus asked His disciples, "Who do you say that I am?" (Matthew 16:15). How would you answer it? Why is this question still relevant today?

2. Jesus transforms those who encounter Him, such as Zacchaeus and the leper. Describe how He has transformed you.

3. Read John 8:12. Reflect on Jesus as the Light of the World. Where is He calling you to walk in greater faith and trust?

4. Write your response to Jesus's question, "Who do you say that I Am?" and describe how your life reflects your response.

For Further Study & Reflection

1. The angelic announcement at Jesus's birth declared peace and goodwill to humanity. What kind of peace did Jesus bring? How does it differ from the world's idea of peace?

2. Read Isaiah 6:1. Isaiah saw the Lord of Hosts seated on a throne, while Jesus was born in a stable. What does this contrast reveal about the nature of God's kingdom?

3. Read Isaiah 9:6. How do these names deepen our understanding of Jesus's identity?

4. Read Revelation 19:11-16. How does this passage contrast with Jesus's first coming?

5. Read Isaiah 11:4-5. How does Isaiah describe how Jesus judges?

6. Jesus is called the Son of David. Why is this title significant? How does it connect to His mission?

The world changed the moment Jesus was born in Bethlehem. His conception, life, and death fulfilled the prophecies in the Old Testament. But another prophecy remains—His Second Coming. Until His return, we are called to walk in faith, live as citizens of His kingdom, and share His light with a darkened world.

7

The Gift

This story is a composite drawn from real accounts shared by missionaries and local believers. While the events are not tied to one person, they reflect the experiences of many who have chosen to follow Christ in the midst of conflict.

The clear mountain air was cool and refreshing as Juan trudged along the narrow trail. The rugged peaks loomed around him, silent witnesses to his journey. His legs ached from the long day, but he pressed on. Nightfall was coming, and he wanted to reach his village before dark.

That afternoon, he had met with a group of men weary from years of fighting. They weren't hardened rebels—just fathers and husbands who had grown tired of the violence and longed for home. Juan spoke to them about a different kind of freedom found through faith in Jesus Christ. Together, they knelt on the forest floor and prayed, their weapons laid aside. At that moment, they chose to leave the guerrilla band and return to their families with a new purpose to love and serve.

As the sun dipped lower, shadows stretched across the trail. Juan's thoughts turned to his family, picturing the joy of seeing his wife and three children after a long day. But just as hope filled his heart, the peaceful silence shattered. Three men burst from the underbrush, their machetes raised high.

Before Juan could react, the first blow fractured his arm. He raised his other arm to shield himself, but the strikes kept coming, tearing through his flesh and bone. "Where is your Jesus now?" one of the attackers mocked.

Juan fell to his knees, blood soaking the trail. In his final moments, he cried out to Jesus, whispering a prayer for deliverance. The pain faded, and he felt a profound peace. Lifted upwards, surrounded by the voices of angels, Juan gave his life for his faith, a martyr for the cause of Christ.

His death was not in vain. The King he served—Jesus, the Lord of Hosts—fights not only against evil but for His people. He is the King who battles for us, even in death, bringing eternal victory.

Preparing for Eternity

Juan's final moments were not the end but the beginning of his eternal reward. His faith reflects the greater truth that despite the suffering in this world, God's promises endure, preparing us for eternity.

A broken world searches for answers to solve the riddle of why humanity cannot save itself or fix the problems that destroy so many lives. The darkness lingers despite the advancement of science and industry.

In Revelation 6:10, the saints in heaven ask God, "How long will You delay before You avenge the blood of the martyrs?" Through Biblical prophecies, the *Lord of Hosts* answers that age-old question. The visionary Isaiah is one of the first to give a true glimpse of the future. He saw how the plan of God's salvation would be carried out. His writings reveal a glorious future with Jesus's return, and all things made new. He saw the redemption of Israel and the light to the gentile nations.

Isaiah records a glimpse into the promises of God as given to him by the Commander of the Heavenly Armies.

> "The wolf also shall dwell with the lamb, and a little child shall lead them. They shall not hurt nor destroy in all My holy mountain. For the earth shall be full of the knowledge of the Lord. And on that day, there shall be a Root of Jesse, who shall stand as a banner to the people." (Isaiah 11:6-10 paraphrased)

In Revelation, the Apostle John expands our understanding of our God-ordained future through the words given to him by the Spirit of prophecy of Jesus Christ. He reveals what was, what is, and what is to come. In the end, Jesus triumphs over all evil. He defeats those who conspire against His holiness–Satan, corrupt systems, and rebellious kings and nations.

When Jesus first comes as the baby born in Bethlehem, conceived by the Holy Spirit in the virgin Mary, He begins the process of salvation as prophesied by Isaiah. Then, Isaiah 61:1-2, quoted by Jesus in Luke 4:18-19, outlines His mission as the Messiah: to preach to the poor, heal the brokenhearted and the blind, and bring freedom to those enslaved by sin.

Jesus came to confront evil in all its forms, fulfilling God's promise. He sets people free from spiritual bondage, addictions, and oppression, bringing both physical and inner healing. Through His justice and truth, He proclaimed the arrival of God's Kingdom, which will ultimately destroy the kingdom of Satan.

Wherever Jesus went, He fulfilled His mission and sent His followers to the nations to spread salvation and make disciples. The seeds of redemption, preparing the way for His return, were sown.

Our Deliverer will complete His mission when He soon returns as the *Lord of Hosts* with His heavenly army. Once all evil and corruption are defeated, God's plan will be finalized. In the end, Jesus gives us a new heaven, earth, and Jerusalem. At that time, we will forever worship Father God and Jesus Christ in the Light of their glory.

Standing with Israel

God's redemptive plan is woven through history, and His covenant with Israel remains central to this unfolding story. As followers of Jesus, we are to do our part to complete His vision of preparing the nations for His return. One way Beverly and I have done this is through our involvement with the Jerusalem Prayer Breakfast (JPB) since its inception. The founder of JPB, Albert Veksler, had a vision of hosting prayer breakfasts under the leadership of the Knesset. The breakfasts are a place where Jews and

Christians unite to pray, develop friendships, and work to fulfill the Genesis 12 promise of God to Abram that those who bless Israel will be blessed and those who curse Israel will be cursed.

I was honored to be on the first JPB Board that helped plan and implement Veksler's vision. During our meetings in Jerusalem, I sensed from the start that this was one of God's plans to prepare the way for the return of Jesus.

JPB's ministry focuses on preparing nations to be sheep nations and not the goat nations Jesus mentioned in Matthew 25. When Our Lord comes to judge the nations, they must meet two criteria. One is that a sheep nation must be in covenant with the God of Abraham through the New Covenant of the blood of Jesus Christ. And that the nations would be judged by whether they treated the Jews with honor, respect, and love, ministering to their needs. Those nations that reject Jesus and His covenant and persecute the Jews are the goat nations, judged guilty of their sins against God and the Jews. They will be separated from the sheep nations to eternal punishment as described in Matthew 25 and Revelation 20.

We started with a yearly prayer breakfast in Jerusalem for world leaders. It was a tremendous success. Next, we expanded the prayer breakfasts to other countries. Beverly and I were blessed to host the first one in the U.S. in Orlando, Florida.

One of the goals of these prayers connecting political, business, and spiritual leaders was to inspire countries to move their embassies in Israel from Tel Aviv to

Jerusalem. Much of the international community views the eastern portion of the city as occupied territory. In its defense during the 1967 Six-Day War, Israel captured East Jerusalem from Jordan. JPB's advocacy aligned with the international discussion on recognizing Jerusalem as Israel's capital. I, along with many others, believe the spiritual momentum contributed to President Trump's decision to move the U.S. embassy in 2018.

In January 2025, Beverly and I had the unique opportunity to join 680 Christian and Jewish leaders from around the world to meet at President Trump's Mar-a-Lago resort in Palm Beach, Florida. Speakers from the Knesset, Congress, such as Michele Bachmann, and other political and business leaders from around the world gave powerful presentations. We heard Israeli leaders describe the horrors of October 7 and the struggles of the war. One of our key prayer focuses was the release of the hostages, and not long after our prayer meetings, some hostages were released.

When we began the JPB in Mar-a-Lago with worship and praise, Jews and Christians singing as one, the Holy Spirit came upon me with such a sense of God's presence that I was moved to tears of joy. We have failed rather miserably to bless the Jews, but God, in His authority, power, and majesty, has done what Isaiah and Jesus prophesied. The Messiah would come to reign over the nations to bring Jews and Gentiles together among the remaining sheep nations in the new heaven and earth.

During one of the meetings, we stood to pray for the nations. I was led to call out Pakistan and Cuba, highlighting the struggles and challenges these nations face, particularly in the areas where we do much of our ministry. Others lifted their nations, addressing urgent needs from Japan to Nigeria to the U.S.

The prayers, the alliances, and the intercession are all part of God's unfolding story. But beyond this moment, what awaits us?

Restoring His Design

Just as God's covenant with Israel stands firm, so does His promise to restore all of creation. What does this restoration look like?

For those who have repented and given their hearts in faith to Christ, the wonder and joy of His kingdom await. Eternity will be experienced there; time as we know it no longer exists. Love, oneness, and glory are restored to their original design. There is no sin, evil, or death for all who believe in Jesus and live God's way.

We will act as we were created to act, to serve one Master. Our nature will no longer be corrupted. We will have resurrected bodies as Jesus did after His resurrection. We will be immortal and live in perfect unity with God, ourselves, and others. There is no inner war of the soul where our flesh rages against the Spirit within us. No sickness, disease, sorrow, or tears. Death will be no more. The holiness of God will be without blemish. We will see and experience wonders we cannot conceive in our present lives. We will know the glory of God in all of His fullness. Now, that is perfect peace.

Our lives will be filled with the worship of God the Father and Jesus Christ. The intimacy of love will be without fear, doubts, or selfish desires. There will be no marriage, and sexual relations will be extinct. Still, we will know the deep satisfaction of rest and peace, which, in this life, is beyond our knowledge.

The image of God in us will be fully restored, enabling us to create with a depth of wisdom and beauty beyond anything we know now. Our creativity, guided by holiness and righteousness, will reflect God's perfection in ways we can't begin to imagine. Because we were made in His image, our restored nature will allow us to build, innovate, and express with a brilliance that surpasses human limitations—not as gods, but as perfected reflections of our Creator.

The question of dominion over the earth will be settled. The world system will be God's kingdom as He originally intended. Jesus Christ will reign with all authority and power. The philosophies and religions of humanity will not exist. There will be one perfect system that reflects the character and virtue of God.

There will be no place for our foolishness. The wisdom and ways of God will teach us His eternal truths. We will know Jesus's sacrifice has reaped the everlasting reward and promise that He won on the cross for all humanity. Joy will abound.

Now, what is to come in our day? Two kingdoms are in conflict. One is the ancient system of Satan that has captured the heart of humanity. The other is the redemptive power of Jesus Christ, which has come to replace the evil and rebellion permeating our world.

Living with Assurance

Matthew 24 and 25 give us a rather descriptive picture of the words of Jesus, confirming what Isaiah and John saw.

A worldwide community that desperately tries to solve its problems without going to war will exist. Yet, humanity cannot help but rise up against each other. War, actual and impending, will be global until the final battle rages to see who will have dominion over the earth. Will communism, capitalism, secular humanism, atheism, or another religion, such as Islam, rule the world? Or does Jesus Christ win the heart of humanity?

In Genesis 1, God gave Adam and Eve dominion over the world as His first blessing. It was a beautiful gift that reflects how God ruled His universe with love, holiness, righteousness, and justice. Unfortunately, Adam sinned. Corruption and rebellion entered the DNA of humanity, causing us to misuse our gift of dominion for our own selfish and prideful purposes. Instead of serving one another in love, we looked to dominate and oppress.

Our long history has moved from local dominion to a superpower that will win the battle for control over how humanity will live. Despite our best efforts to live in peace, we create chaos that leads to wars, division, and oppression. The solutions we devise only lead to more turmoil and suffering.

Why do we continue to act against God's laws with our choices? Why do we still enslave men, women, and children in sex trafficking? Why do the ongoing injustices of illicit drugs and forced labor continue to exist? Why do so many people hate the Jews? Why have they been persecuted since the call of Abraham? Why do nations seek to wipe Israel from the face of the earth? Why does it often feel like we are on the brink of World War III despite living in an age of advanced technology and supposed enlightenment?

Isaiah saw an age of unity, void of evil and conflict. There was peace with an everlasting government led by the Child born to us, Jesus Christ, as King.

Global events such as pandemics, economic downturns, AI disruptions, wars, earthquakes, and famines often overwhelm us. Adding to this are the rapid technological advances that isolate individuals and the replacement of God's laws with those of humanity. Love grows cold, marriage is dismissed as unnecessary, and false teachings thrive in an age of widespread deception.

The spirit of the antichrist gains influence, leading the world into a renewed worship of the ancient gods. Meanwhile, humanity constantly struggles over who will have dominion on Earth. These forces, both seen and unseen, shape the direction of our world in ways that can feel chaotic and disorienting.

The rise of idolatry takes form in four major sins, as prophesied in Revelation:

1. A spirit of murder (Revelation 9:21a): "Nor did they repent of their murders..."

2. The use of drugs to find peace and happiness to connect with the gods (Revelation 9:21b): "...their magic arts..." (magic arts is translated from the Greek word "pharmakeia," which refers to the use of drugs or potions associated with occult and idolatrous practices).
3. Sexual perversion will become accepted as a normal lifestyle (Revelation 9:21c): "...their sexual immorality..."
4. Theft will become global through computers and technology, as well as the rejection of laws that protect property (Revelation 9:21d): "...or their thefts."

Yet, the spread of Christianity to the nations will continue while Israel will continue to be a focal point in world events. Despite the turbulence, the *Lord of Hosts* protects the followers of Jesus and the Jewish people. We can live with His peace and without fear because of the assurance of eternal life over the temporary life in this world system, which the Bible calls Babylon.

Turning from Evil

Even as we live in the assurance of Christ's victory, we must recognize the ongoing battle for truth and righteousness. Satan and his demons continue to try to destroy our families and households. Nevertheless, many people will be more interested in the temporary of this world, neglecting the eternal call of God.

The followers of Jesus will become divided. There will be a continued falling away from His teachings as many turn to secular humanism and its promises of self-fulfillment, surrounding themselves with voices that tell them what they want to hear, not what they need to hear (2 Timothy 4:3–4). Though many will claim to follow Jesus and even call Him "Lord," their lives will tell a different story. He will say to them, "I never knew you" (Matthew 7:21–23). Even among those who once had a personal relationship with Him, some will grow fearful and cling to their resources, hoarding the blessings of God. But others will remain faithful, resisting the pull of self-preservation and self-focus. They will give freely, using their possessions to advance the Kingdom of Jesus Christ.

In the end, nations will rise against nations, especially against Israel. When all seems hopeless, Jesus will come with His armies of heaven to defeat Satan and the leaders of armies in rebellion against God and Israel.

In Matthew 25:31-46, Jesus describes His return in glory when He will separate the nations like a shepherd separates the sheep from the goats. The sheep represent those who followed His will by showing compassion and care to others, while the goats represent those who failed to do so, rejecting God's love and mercy. In particular, verses 41-46 describe the judgment of the goats, who are condemned for their lack of love and righteous actions.

Thus, Jesus will vanquish all that is vile and conduct a final judgment against the goat nations who rejected the blood covenant of Jesus Christ and persecuted the Jews. All the people who rejected God's love and salvation through Jesus will be sentenced to the lake of fire, eternal separation from God.

Because they decided over and over to reject the *Lord of Hosts,* all of humanity who rejected Him will share in the same fate as Satan and his demons. No hope. No love. Everything God offered them in the Covenant of Abraham and the New Covenant of Jesus Christ will be out of their reach forever. Those who remained faithful to the end will, like Jesus, receive resurrected bodies. Then, as promised by the Prophets, they will live in His eternal age. There will be a new heaven and earth, free from sin and evil. In this kingdom, the sheep nations, with Israel as their leader, will be governed by Christ.

In Isaiah Chapters 61-66, the revelation of the preparation for the coming eternal age begins with the Messiah's job description during His first coming. It then moves to the last days when Israel rebuilds the ruins, and the good news of salvation is known throughout the globe. Zion will no longer be desolate or forsaken. It will be the crown of God's glory, and Jerusalem will be the home of God's holy people. The Land of Promise will be a light; the nations will seek it out.

The judgment will be upon the surrounding nations that make war on Israel. We see this unfolding before our eyes. Israel, surrounded by unfriendly neighbors and terrorist armies, fights for its life daily. The Scriptures speak clearly of judgment against all who wage war on Israel, including those leading nations and groups such as Iran, Hamas, and Hezbollah. These warnings are not political statements but divine truths, calling even the fiercest enemies to repentance before the day of the Lord.

God protects Israel despite its rebellion, acting to save it solely out of His love. The Jewish people will eventually cry out to God to save them from their sins and enemies. They will call to the *Lord of Hosts* to deliver them, just as Revelation ends with our call for Jesus to come.

Isaiah Chapter 65 decrees the righteous judgment of God for those who did not seek Him, but He still acted to save His rebellious people. He will honor His promise to Abraham and his descendants. In the end, they will rejoice as they inherit all of God's promises in His covenant.

"For behold, I create new heavens and a new earth..." These words are reaffirmed in Revelation Chapters 21 and 22 as Jesus ushers in the renewed creation, fulfilling God's ultimate promise of restoration.

Enduring through Trials

Though the forces of darkness wage war against truth, God's promises endure. Nowhere is this more evident than in the story of Israel—a nation forged through suffering and sustained by divine providence.

In Isaiah 66:8, we are told that Israel would be born in a day—a prophecy fulfilled in 1948. But its ongoing trials are like a refining fire that purifies and prepares the nation for God's ultimate glory. Israel's birth is part of a process spanning over a century of aliyah (Jewish immigration to the land), multiple wars, and the restoration of Jerusalem as Israel's capital in 1967. Since 1948, Israel has endured constant warfare, including the War of Independence (1948-1949), the Six-Day War (1967), the Yom Kippur War (1973), and the surprise October 7, 2023 attack. This struggle will continue until the return of Jesus Christ.

The pains of these trials—wars, persecutions, and unrest—are like the intense heat of refinement necessary for shaping Israel for God's ultimate plan. God will vindicate Israel and come as the *Lord of Hosts*, Jesus the Messiah, to save it. The nations will see His glory and come to Jerusalem in worship. Our Savior will reign, granting eternal life to the faithful and rendering eternal judgment to those who never repented.

Jesus creates the new heaven and earth for those who are the faithful remnant of Abraham. However, for those who rejected the Messiah, "their worm does not die, and their fire is not quenched..." Jesus quotes this verse in Mark 9:42-50 to illustrate the eternal consequences of sinful choices that lead to hell.

Isaiah saw the *Lord of Hosts*. He was given the message to repent and return to love and worship the one true living God of Abraham. The promise of God to redeem and restore His creation will become a reality for those who have received His offer and promise of life.

We will kneel and worship our King Jesus, the Son of David, and enjoy His blessings and love, for there will be no more curse of sin and death. We will learn and discover God's greater plan for us in the coming age. No fear but faith and hope in Jesus Christ.

Waiting for His Return

When will this happen? The Bible is clear from the words of Jesus to His disciples; no one knows the day or hour, but He expects us to know the season of His return. That season is now. It began in 1967 when Jerusalem was retaken as the capital of Israel. Jesus prophesied that He would return within one generation when the Gentiles no longer trampled Jerusalem. Gentiles have oppressed Jerusalem beginning with its fall to Babylon 2600 years ago, up until its restoration as Israel's capital.

The question then is how long a generation is, which determines the length of our season of preparing the way for His Second Coming. We do not know. It can't be forty years, for that time has passed. Seventy years could be a good educated guess. The Jews came out of bondage in Babylon to return to Jerusalem after 70 years, as prophesied by Jeremiah and confirmed by Daniel. That would give us a date around 2037, but I must emphasize that we won't know the exact year.

A generation can be a hundred years or the span of Methuselah, who lived 969 years. Based on world events and societal changes, I predict 70 years, but to be clear, no one knows. We should live as though Jesus were coming today. "Watch" because Jesus cautioned in Matthew 24:42 and 25:13 that we will not know when He will return.

I know one thing: in God's time, His return is imminent, as I have shared in my testimony about when the Spirit spoke to me about Jesus's coming again. I was to go to the nations, the church, and Israel to call people to repent and believe in

Jesus, to be baptized with the Holy Spirit and with fire, and to take up their cross, deny self, and follow Jesus.

Wake up! The King is coming. He is on His white stallion, prepared to return. His arrival is imminent—are you ready?

"Come, Lord Jesus, come!" must be the prayer of Christ's Body as commanded in Revelation 22:20. When He comes in His glory with His angels and the trumpet sounds, everyone will answer the question: "Who do you say that I am?"

He is Jesus Christ, the *Lord of Hosts*, the Prince of Peace, the Alpha and Omega, the only One worthy of our praise, the Lord and Savior, our Deliverer, the King of kings, and the Lord of lords. In Him alone will we trust.

Today is the day of salvation. Jesus tells us to ask, seek, and knock with a hunger for Him and a desperation to be like Him. God, restore me to how you created me before I was ever conceived in my mother's womb is the cry of the Psalmist.

> "My frame was not hidden from you
> when I was made in the secret place,
> when I was woven together
> in the depths of the earth.
> Your eyes saw my unformed body;
> all the days ordained for me
> were written in your book
> before one of them came to be."
> (Psalm 139:15-16).

Accepting His Gift

- God has a singular gift for you, with three aspects of blessings:
- The gift of eternal life is to know and love Jesus forever.
- The gift of a new vision for living to prepare the way for His return.
- The gift of a glorious future that spans beyond eternity.

Jesus Christ will fulfill all of God's promises. The Prince of Peace delights in giving us the gift of the New Covenant. Open your heart to Jesus and pray to receive the fullness of this gift so that you can use your life for His glory. Believe and receive. Tell Him, here am I, send me, empower me, give me dreams and visions to fulfill Your vision to prepare the way for Your return. I love you, Jesus, with all of my heart. I trust in You alone.

This gift is freely given, but time is short. The question remains: *Are you ready?*

GOING DEEPER | Chapter 7

Reflect & Respond

1. As followers of Christ, we are called to prepare for the return of the Lord of Hosts. What steps can you take this week to align your life with His purposes?

2. Reflect on Revelation 22:20—"Come, Lord Jesus!" How can you develop a greater longing for His return? How can you live with the anticipation of His return in your daily walk?

3. The Lord of Hosts is often described as a defender and protector of His people, yet Juan was brutally attacked and killed for his faith. How does this seeming contradiction challenge or deepen your understanding of God? How does Scripture reconcile God's justice and ultimate victory with the suffering of His faithful servants?

4. How does the description of Jesus as the Alpha and Omega impact your understanding of the Lord of Hosts reigning over history and the future?

For Further Study & Reflection

1. Read Isaiah 11:6-10. What does this prophecy reveal about the transformation the Lord of Hosts will bring when He returns?

2. Isaiah saw the Lord of Hosts in His glory, and John received the Revelation of Jesus's final victory. How do these visions give assurance amid global chaos and uncertainty?

3. Read Genesis 12:3. How does it support the importance of blessing Israel? How does this relate to God's covenant with Abraham?

4. Read Matthew 25:32-36. What distinguishes sheep nations from goat nations? Why does the Lord of Hosts judge nations based on their relationship with Jesus and Israel?

5. Throughout history, Israel has been surrounded by enemies and faced constant opposition. How does Isaiah's prophecy about Zion's restoration in Isaiah 62 provide hope for the future of Israel?

6. Read Matthew 24:3-31. What are some of the signs Jesus described in Matthew 24 that indicate His return is near?

Even though Jesus Christ reigns, we live in a world of conflict. While the battle between light and dark continues, so does the call. Those who have encountered the *Lord of Hosts* and carry His Spirit are called to take action. History is still being written through lives fully surrendered to the King of Kings, the Commander of the Armies.

8

The Final Word:
The *Lord of Hosts* Is Coming

Throughout this book, you've read stories drawn from real lives, stories of surrender, sacrifice, and bold faith. These accounts, combined with the truth of Scripture, have pointed to one central reality: *Jesus Christ is the Lord of Hosts*, the Commander of Heaven's armies. He fights for His people, fulfills every promise, and will return in glory to reign forever.

We have followed the prophetic thread from Isaiah's vision to the final chapters of Revelation. We've seen God's plan unfold through Israel, the Church, and the nations. The signs of the times are not hidden—they are written plainly for those who are watching and willing to prepare.

This is not the time for passive belief.

It is the time for repentance, holiness, and courageous obedience.

It is the time to stand with Israel, proclaim the gospel, and live with eyes fixed on eternity.

We are called to watch, pray, and prepare. To live as those who carry the banner of the King. To reject the compromise of this world and declare the Lordship of Jesus over every area of our lives.

The *Lord of Hosts* is coming—not as a baby in a manger, but as the righteous Judge and conquering King.

He will separate the sheep from the goats.

He will restore all that was broken.

And He will dwell with His people in a new heaven and a new earth.

Let this truth ignite urgency in your spirit.

Let it draw you to your knees in worship.

Let it shape how you live each day.

He is coming. He is worthy. And He is calling.

Will you answer?

EPILOGUE: MORE WORDS OF INSPIRATION

Little did I know that my second mission to Israel would dramatically change my life. In 2008, Beverly and I took 30 people to experience the Land of Promise. We hoped that we would all connect with God's vision for the future of Israel and our own Jesus-given vision for how we could be a part of fulfilling His global plan of redemption.

We had no idea God had a special mission for us in Israel. As our journey unfolded, I remember asking why we were going all the way to Eilat, a city at the southern tip of Israel. The answer did not come until several days later.

We traveled back up to Jerusalem and then to the Sea of Galilee. At every stop we made, we prayed for the Holy Spirit to be poured out upon Israel and her people. It was my firm conviction that Jesus and the Father had sent the Holy Spirit on the Day of Pentecost. I believed the final outpouring of the Spirit before Jesus returned would happen in Jerusalem.

During each session of prayer and worship, we experienced a powerful move from the Holy Spirit. At the end of our visit, I realized we had prayed at seven locations throughout the nation, from Eilat in the south to Jerusalem in the north. We didn't plan to do this, but the Spirit of God led us to the sevenfold complete acts of prayer in seven vital locations. I was overwhelmed by what God had us experience.

When I returned to Orlando, I was soaring in the heavenlies with faith and a deeper understanding of my call to Israel. On the first Friday at home, I spent three hours in prayer and study when suddenly the Spirit spoke to me to go on my daily run. Surprised but ready for a break, I changed into running gear and took off on a two-mile jog toward the canal near my home. I loved the canal portion of my run as I often saw gators, otters, birds, fish, and, once in a while, a snake.

Partway through the scenic route, the Holy Spirit began speaking to me. His voice was so clear I stopped running to focus on what He was saying.

"The return of My Son, Jesus Christ, is imminent. I am sending you to the nations, to the church, and Israel. Call the people to repent and believe in Jesus as their Savior. Pray for them to be baptized in the Holy Spirit, and to deny themselves, take up their cross, and follow Jesus."

What did 'imminent' mean? The force of this message left me awestruck. I tried to grasp its meaning. Later, I realized that the train had already left the station—it was in motion. I didn't know exactly when it would arrive, but I knew it was coming soon. Soon, in God's time, not mine. *"A thousand years is but a day to God."*

Was I meant to fulfill God's message within the church I pastored? I had been at Pine Castle United Methodist Church in Orlando for 16 years—seven as the associate pastor and evangelist and nine as the senior pastor. We had just built a beautiful sanctuary and had a thriving 700-student school. How could I go to the nations and do all God seemed to ask?

The answer was that I was to retire from the Methodist Florida Conference and become a full-time evangelist. I was to *go* from what was familiar to a new land–one with no salary, no health insurance, and no future income. Fortunately, we had a nice home, but how could we afford it?

After discussing all of this with Beverly, we agreed that I should become an evangelist and retire from the Methodist Church. We needed to put our full trust in God and step out of the boat in faith. A week later, we were in Washington, D.C., for a Right to Life Rally. While Beverly and I strolled through the crowd of thousands, we ran into a good friend, Alex Clattenburg, a pastor in the Orlando area. Alex said he had a word for us and asked if he could pray over us. He had no idea about what Beverly and I had decided.

His prayer was that we would start a new church within 60 days. Wow! No one can do that in two months. Plus, I told him I was going into full-time evangelism and that I would not be starting a church. He replied, "I prayed for what I believe the Spirit spoke to me for you."

Alex planted a seed on what we should do. However, that Sunday evening, Beverly and I agreed that we would go forward with our original plan for retirement and evangelism. However, God had other plans.

Monday morning, while in my office, several men from my church came to speak to me. They shared that they couldn't stay in the Methodist Church due to differences in their understanding of God's Word and the direction in which the Methodist Conference was heading. I then shared my plan of going into full-time evangelism. The men offered that if I helped them plant a new church, they would help me do all the evangelism I was led to do. After much prayer, we agreed that it was God's plan. Within 60 days, I retired from the Methodist Conference, and we started Global Revolution Church.

Yes, Global Revolution was quite a radical name because we believed God would use us to spark worldwide reformation of His church. Lofty ideals. Today, I laugh at our naive plans. Yet, we were serious in our intent to follow Jesus and to get back to the Biblical truth. So, I began to focus on helping start this new church while fulfilling my call as an evangelist. All of these plans were anchored in Jesus Christ with the intent of sharing with people to get ready; the return of Jesus was imminent.

Beverly and I started a television ministry based on the teachings of Jesus's return, which was going quite well until God gave us another surprise about eight months later. Through Beverly's online prayer ministry, a 16-year-old Ohio girl, Rifqa Bary, reached out to her. Rifqa was from a Muslim family but had secretly given her life to Jesus. She was fearful that she would be the victim of an honor killing for becoming a Christian.

We knew the decision to protect Rifqa would affect our lives, but we had no idea how profoundly. It led us on a journey of faith that would bring us to our knees in deeper surrender to Jesus. We gave Rifqa a safe haven in our home. The story made the national and even world news. Because we decided to protect her life, some of the church leadership shut us out of the church one Sunday morning. We lost all we had built up in our short time at Global

Revolution Church. However, 90% of the congregation chose to stay with us during this trying time.

Our money, building, TV ministry, and reputation were all gone. The news media at first hailed us as heroes, which we were not. We simply believed God called us to save Rifqa's life, which we did with the help of many others. Then, the full force of Muslim activists came against us, and only by the grace of God and the love of our body of believers did we survive.

The media crucified us for saving Rifqa. Friends turned against us. We went from heroes to villains with accusations that we were kidnapping, child-molesting brainwashers who used drugs.

In the midst of this turmoil, we launched a new church, Encounter, with our people. A friend, Bill Blakely, offered us his business space to hold Sunday worship. As a result, we never missed a Sunday of worship. My missionary friend, Delbert from Zambia, loved meeting with us in that setting. He felt like we were the early believers worshiping in a secret hideout while being persecuted weekly by the media and Muslim activists.

Rifqa was eventually taken into custody and two days later released into foster care. You can read Rifqa's story in her New York Times best-selling book, *Hiding in the Light*. I included some of what we experienced alongside Rifqa in my novel, *Greater Love*. (The novel puts into story form my global experiences and calling to wake up the nations about Jesus's return.)

Sixteen years later, God has made the vision He gave me a reality. Two years ago, after a powerful move by God on an evangelism trip to Cuba, God led us to launch the World Evangelism Center (WEC) in Orlando.

Immediately, people who I had partnered with in missions and evangelism, plus new people across the globe, joined us in our Spirit-led vision that was given. We have directors from five continents and amazing partners. We are seeing a global revolution for Jesus that surpasses my imagination.

I am overwhelmed with joy by the reports and ministries of what God is doing through our partners and through what we are doing at WEC Orlando. Visit our website at worldevangelismcenterorlando.org to get a glimpse of what God is doing to prepare the way for His Son's imminent return.

We have ministered for Jesus in 188 nations through my *Awaken* podcast, television ministries, crusades, conferences, church partnerships, and ministry partners. We estimate at least 10,000 people a month come to Christ as Savior. Thousands more are baptized with the Holy Spirit, and we are told of miracle healings, signs, and wonders. People are taking up their cross, denying themselves to follow Jesus and prepare for His return.

I confess I am living the dream Jesus gave me. He has expanded upon it from my first encounter in 1980. I didn't understand at the time that His purpose was to take my life and use it for His glory. But He made it clear—I would go to the nations to proclaim that God became a man, died on the cross for our sins, rose from the dead, ascended to heaven, and will return soon. His love offers a new vision for life.

My last words for you: Jesus is the only One to trust completely for your eternal destiny. He is preparing the world for His return. When He returns, there will be no time to repent and believe in Him. It will all happen in the twinkling of an eye. It is the reason why Christians must take their calling seriously. Jesus loves everyone and wants them to spend eternity with Him in the glory and wonder of His Presence.

If you have not already done so, give Jesus your heart and surrender to Him as your Lord and Savior. Ask for forgiveness of your sins, turn away from your old vision of living, and receive His new vision for your life. Believe in Him alone for your redemption and receive His free gift of eternal life. Pray to be baptized with the Holy Spirit. To be God's witness and to receive His visions and dreams for your life. Take up your cross, deny yourself, and follow Jesus.

You will become part of the greatest movement in the history of the world.

The *Lord of Hosts* loves you, and I love you!

ENDNOTES

Chapter 1

1. Newhouse, Alana, and Jeremy Stern. "Hamas's War on Israel: Everything You Need to Know." *The Free Press*, October 9, 2023. Hamas War on Israel: Everything You Need to Know.

2. TOI Staff. "Israel Revises Death Toll from Oct. 7 Hamas Assault, Dropping It from 1,400 to 1,200." *The Times of Israel*, November 11, 2023. Israel revises death toll from Oct. 7 Hamas assault, dropping it from 1,400 to 1,200 | The Times of Israel.

3. Newhouse

4. "Israel Revises Death Toll," *The Times of Israel.*

5. TOI Staff. "Death Toll from Nova Music Festival Massacre on Oct. 7 Raised by 100 to Over 360." *The Times of Israel*, November 18, 2023. Death toll from Nova music festival massacre on Oct. 7 raised by 100 to over 360 | The Times of Israel.

6. "Hamas Roasted Babies in Ovens,' Says Israel Emergency Services Worker Who Saw Aftermath of Massacre." *LBC*, November 2, 2023. 'Hamas roasted babies in ovens,' says Israel emergency services worker who saw aftermath... - LBC.

7. McCall, Tom. "Asbury Professor: We're Witnessing a 'Surprising Work of God'." *Christianity Today*, February 13, 2023. Asbury Professor: We're Witnessing a 'Surprising Work of God' - Christianity Today.

Chapter 2

1. Barna Group. "Church Dropouts Have Risen to 64%—But What About Those Who Stay?" September 4, 2019. Church Dropouts Have Risen to 64%—But What About Those Who Stay? - Barna Group.

2. Pew Research Center. "In U.S., Decline of Christianity Continues at Rapid Pace." October 17, 2019. In U.S., Decline of Christianity Continues at Rapid Pace | Pew Research Center.

3. Wildenberg, Lara. "Generation Z Turn to Astrology 'to Answer Life's Big Questions.'" *The Times*, January 19, 2025. Generation Z turn to astrology 'to answer life's big questions'.

4. Hall, Richard, and Andrew Feinberg. "Netanyahu Cancels Washington Visit after US Abstains on Gaza Ceasefire Vote at UN." *The Independent*, March 25, 2024. UN passes resolution calling for ceasefire in Gaza as US abstains | The Independent.

Chapter 5

1. Kaye, Ephraim. "Desecraters of Memory: Confronting Holocaust Denial." *Jewish Virtual Library*, Yad Vashem

— International School of Holocaust Studies, 1997. Hitler's Threats Against the Jews (1941-1945).

2. TOI Staff, "Full Official Record: What the Mufti Said to Hitler," *The Times of Israel*, October 21, 2015. https://www.timesofisrael.com/full-official-record-what-the-mufti-said-to-hitler/.

3. Ephraim

Chapter 6

1. Lidman, Melanie. "Hamas Turns Over the Remains Said to Be of a Mother and Her 2 Young Children." *NBC Philadelphia*, February 20, 2025. Hamas turns over the remains said to be of a mother, her children – NBC10 Philadelphia.

MEET THE AUTHOR

Blake Lorenz has dedicated his life to following Jesus and inviting others to do the same. A former professional baseball player turned pastor and evangelist, Blake has preached across five continents, helped plant more than 700 churches, and led thousands to Christ. He is the founder of the World Evangelism Center Orlando and formerly served on the board of the Jerusalem Prayer Breakfast.

Blake and his wife, Beverly, have been partners in life and ministry for over forty years. They have three children and eight grandchildren who bring them great joy. Blake's passion for the return of Christ fuels both his preaching and his writing, including his novel *Greater Love*—a prophetic story of calling, redemption, and the coming King.

MAKING A DIFFERENCE:
WORLD EVANGELISM CENTER ORLANDO

Every book you purchase makes a difference.

All net proceeds from this book go directly to support the work of **World Evangelism Center Orlando**, whose mission is to prepare the way for Jesus's Second Coming by calling people to repent and believe in Jesus Christ, to be baptized with the Holy Spirit and fire, and to follow Him fully. Their vision is to go to the church, to Israel, and to the nations establishing World Evangelism Centers around the globe—planting churches, spreading the salvation of Jesus Christ, and helping all believers walk in the power of the Holy Spirit.

Your support helps carry that mission forward.

Want to Multiply the Impact?

If this book spoke to you, consider sharing it with others. Whether it's for a small group, a book club, a ministry outreach, or simply to encourage friends and family, bulk orders help us extend the mission even further.

For Bulk Orders (10 or more):

Special pricing is available for supporters who wish to order 10 or more copies. To learn more, email info@worldevangelismcenterorlando.org.

We'd love to partner with you in spreading the message.

ACKNOWLEDGMENTS

"I thank my God upon every remembrance of you."
Philippians 1:3

To those who encouraged, challenged, and contributed to the creation of this book—thank you. Your insights, prayers, and unwavering support made this journey possible. May the impact of your kindness extend far beyond these pages.

Beverly Lorenz

Chris Bright

John Castino

Mary Boza Crimmins

David Hall

Dan Hillman

June Hillman

Paul Holdren

Linda Knight

Sandra Martin

Stan Moore

DON'T MISS BLAKE'S END-TIME THRILLER

Scan the QR code to order *Greater Love*, Blake Lorenz's gripping novel of time travel, romance, and the triumphant return of Jesus Christ. Follow John Nova—former pro athlete turned Spirit-empowered messenger—as he journeys through time to help prepare Israel and the world for the King of kings.

Blending action, romance, biblical truth, and a powerful glimpse into what's coming, *Greater Love* offers a powerful glimpse into what's coming—and why it matters now.

Available on Amazon

PLEASE REVIEW THIS BOOK

Thank you for reading *Jesus, Lord of Hosts.*

If you benefited from this book, I'd be so grateful if you'd take a moment to leave a review. Your words—just a sentence or two—can help others discover the book and be impacted by its message.

You can leave a review on Amazon or wherever you enjoy sharing book recommendations.

Thank you so much for your support!

Made in the USA
Columbia, SC
17 September 2025